RINGING BELLS
IN MALTA

Ringing Bells in Malta

Otto Henry

Copyright © 2016 by Otto Henry.

Library of Congress Control Number:		2016916049
ISBN:	Hardcover	978-1-5245-4601-4
	Softcover	978-1-5245-4600-7
	eBook	978-1-5245-4599-4

All rights reserved. No part of this book may be reproduced or transmitted in any form or by any means, electronic or mechanical, including photocopying, recording, or by any information storage and retrieval system, without permission in writing from the copyright owner.

Any people depicted in stock imagery provided by Thinkstock are models, and such images are being used for illustrative purposes only. Certain stock imagery © Thinkstock.

Print information available on the last page.

Rev. date: 11/10/2016

To order additional copies of this book, contact:
Xlibris
1-888-795-4274
www.Xlibris.com
Orders@Xlibris.com
741549

"Happy he, who, like Ulysses, a glorious voyage made."
Joachim du Bellouy, 1522-1560

An Introduction: March 7, 2016

These are rough anthropological field notes that document my 1972 journey to the Mediterranean island of Malta, in the company of my (then) friends and colleagues "N" (Norma McLeod) and "M" (Marcia Herndon). My main interest in this case was in acquiring ethno-musicological fieldwork experience to augment and justify my teaching in that field at the School of Music, East Carolina University in Greenville, N.C., where I was newly appointed Assistant Professor of Musicology and Composition. I had just completed my Ph.D at Tulane University, New Orleans, where I had briefly studied Ethnomusicology under Dr. McLeod as a secondary interest. Marcia Herndon was a friend and a fellow classmate there.

That said, there were other more complicated reasons behind Norma and Marcia's invitation to accompany them to Malta. Marcia had been there the summer before, gathering materials for her dissertation on Maltese folk singers. Norma had travelled with her. Now they were returning, more for a vacation than anything else.

God bless them, and I didn't care, we were friends together and I didn't mind carrying around a lot of heavy luggage, tape decks, and equipment and posing as "Mr. McLeod" every once in a while!

Another reason was the fact that my wife and I were breaking up, sad as it seems, and now was a good time to get out of the house and out of town. I think that was partially the reason M & N invited me along, a very kind thing to do, I thought. As it turned out, wife was a very talented librarian. A former dean, now out at North Western, hired her to come to Chicago, so she had left before I returned.

Sadly though, (and I regret many times the way it happened, although I don't know how it could have been avoided) Norma got very angry with me because I was late getting our one rented car back in time for her dinner party with some elderly English ladies. I had been delayed, by a priest who was an authority on a bell system I was researching (and you don't just walk away from a priest in Malta!). Also, I had excused myself after dinner to type up my findings, to which Norma took great offense, and she really bawled me out.

Well, there it was! I tried to be calm and apologized, but she would have none of it. Marcia had warned me that Norma often rejected her students. Several had fled her in the middle of training. Maybe it is unfair to mention it, but one had even committed suicide. However, I just took it and swallowed my pride. Marcia offered to help me leave and just go home, but I stuck it out. Relations were strained from then on, and although we spent a week in London before going back to New Orleans, things between us were very cold, and afterwards we just ignored each other at conventions and reunions.

Anyway, the effort was justified. I completed my studies and afterwards, I was able to train and advise students who wanted to study and do ethno-musicological field work.

And I got a heck of a kick out of the bells ringing in Malta!

Prologue: April 2016

Rather than bump into the middle of my field notes that begin upon my arrival in Malta in 1972, it seems best to offer some history for continuity's sake. And to certify that all of this is true and that once I found my direction, I really did climb into every available bell tower I possibly could, named the bells and tried to find out how they were used. Other than that, I hung out with some anthropologists, some folk singers, a lot of Catholic priests, some boat builders, and consequently was dragged to about every fireworks display, church and bar in Malta. I loved it!

It was late in May 1972, when I left my home in Greenville, N.C. to pick up Marcia Herndon at her home in Canton (west of Asheville) and drive thence to New Orleans the following day. Things were tense everywhere. Marcia's family did not approve of her association with her major professor and friend, anthropologist. Dr. Norma McLeod. She and Marcia had already spent several summers in Malta and Marcia was able to complete her PhD dissertation on the folk singing there. I was going through a divorce back at my home. The three of us had been able to get plane tickets to Amsterdam through the Tulane University Alumni Society. We stayed at Norma's place several days and then left New Orleans to fly to Amsterdam.

Well, we had a ball. Norma was an experienced traveler and arranged for separate rooms for me and showed us around the town for a day before we got up early one morning and took off for Zurich, Switzerland. Norma was convinced that we could get more favorable exchange rates there for dollars to Maltese pounds. She was wrong. The three of us had walked into this Swiss bank and were studiously ignored for five or ten minutes until Norma (who had a very loud stentorian voice from years of lecturing) belted out: "Is there no one here to serve the public?" This produced a large comical scrambling of accountants and clerks to the counter. But it turned out they didn't have any Maltese pounds at all. However, we had a very fun time together there. I got sick from drinking too much strong European coffee and was accosted by many attractive prostitutes! Also, we had to leave early in the morning and all the hotel doors had been locked. The staff had gone home, no one stayed the night! I was able to force a basement door open and so we escaped into an alley beside the hotel. From thence we flew to Malta on June 2nd, (with a stopover in Rome!) and were greeted there by singer Johnny Scicluna and his family, where my field notes begin.

Foto 1: Marsaxloxx harbor

The Field Notes

We flew from Switzerland via Rome and landed in Malta around 2 p.m. Our small plane flew around and approached the island from the South, so it did resemble a large whale, tail to the left and kicking the small island of Gozo up to the Northwest. What appeared as a small Band-Aid on the whale's belly was the landing filed, that (fortunately) grew larger as we landed.

It was **Friday, June 2nd**, 1972. I was accompanying my friends and colleagues Dr. Norma McLeod and Dr. Marcia Herndon. Marcia had been to Malta the year with Norma, to finish her dissertation in Ethnomusicology and was returning mainly for a vacation and to tie up some loose ends.

I had also studied with Norma at Tulane University, but I had been able to land a (dream!) job at East Carolina University and finish my dissertation there in a different field. Now here was an opportunity to explore and do field work in Ethno, something Norma was trying to encourage.

Anyway, we gathered our luggage and proceeded through customs. Norma's bag caused some delay and I crossed my fingers because Norma was getting mad and was about to start her "my dear fellow…" routine, but it turned out well anyway. Finally, we were ushered out to the waiting room where we were joyfully greeted by what seemed to be a whole Maltese family whom I learned later were

Johnny Scicluna, his wife, Paula, Paula's sister, Mary and Mary's young son, Paulo.

The women greeted each other affectionately, hugs, etc. Johnny shook hands with me and helped take the luggage out to a small car. We learned later he had rented the car, which was very nice of him because it was very expensive. Johnny a handsome fellow, tanned and able, slender hips, black hair, plain jeans and work shirt. We piled into the car somehow and drove out from the airport into the country side, on he left of the small, slick tarred roads and between stone walls that guarded barren fields and small square houses. In the distance, tall golden domes of churches and cathedrals were everywhere. There were only a few small trees; bent and flat on top.

Johnny drives with great gusto, from the right side of the seat. Malta has been under British control since Napoleon was kicked out of Egypt (and Malta). The Maltese language is a dialect of Arabic but uses the Western alphabet. Just about everyone (he tells me) speaks English, and they use the British money style of a pound, shilling and pence, which, however, was just now converting into a new formula (and causing everyone a lot of confusion).

Soon we arrive at our destination, the small village of Marsaxlokk, where Marcia and Norma had stayed during 1968-1969. The "x" in Maltese, I learn, is an "s" or "sh" sound. The name means "bay of the south west." Several miles to the North lies a companion village called Marsaskala, "Bay of the Northwest." Both are fishing villages built with docks along one side of a large inlet. Although powered by modern gasoline engines, the fishing boats look like ancient Egyptian-Roman ships with tall prows and painted in bright red, yellow and blue. The smaller boats are tied up along the dock, called the "quay" (pronounced "key" – I don't know why). The larger boats are anchored out in the water nearby. All the boats I remember seeing were fitted with carved wooden "eyes" on either side of the bow. As we drove past the large ornate village church at the end of the bay and turned into the road along the quay where the ships were tied up, I thought I had entered a motion picture set, or had gone through a time warp into antiquity!

Foto 2: Boat with "eyes", St. George and a Mermaid

The houses along the quay were small two-story affairs with painted front doors, open, curtained windows and flat roofs, all joined side to side down the front of the quay intermingled with small bars, and one police station in the middle. Arrangements had already been made to sub-let a house belonging to a British officer who had retired there. In fact, I learned that many British colonial people had homes here, rather than live in stormy England, especially Catholics, as Malta was totally Catholic island despite its Arabic roots.

We stopped at Tony's Aviator Bar on the corner to get the house keys from a gentleman-manager named Edgar and drove down the Quay and took a right on Pope Pius V St. up a hill and left on what was called the "New Street off Pope Pius V St." over to our nice two-story rental overlooking the Quay and the water.

The house, called "Tokai," was well furnished and we settled in quickly. I claimed a room at the top of the stairs with an open window to the right. Norma and Marcia settled down the hall a ways. I unpacked and changed clothes. Johnny had left to return his rental car.

Soon Edgar returned with Mr. French and our own rental car. Then we had to turn around and drive back to his garage near Valletta and then go shopping for food in the only Maltese "Supermarket," near Sliema. No paper bags- Marcia brought some cloth carryalls! Drive back to Marsaxlokk. Marcia and Norma take off somewhere, so I make a sandwich and relax for a while. Norma soon returns and takes me next door to meet Joan Grundy, our stout middle-aged English neighbor. Joan has two guests, who leave in a while. I am given two brandies and feeling good. We return next door along with Joan to find Johnny S. had arrived on his motor scooter with wife, Paula, along with a gallon jug of wine. Marcia departs to get us some fish and chips. The rest of us relax in the front room with Johnny's wine. Some discussion of politics I don't understand so I ask for 2nd glass of wine. Johnny is pleased, very happy that Norma, especially, is back. Norma (also) gets looped.

    I was very much taken with Johnny and his wife, Paula. They came across as good, honest country people, generous and friendly. Paula, usually quiet while Johnny is talking, sits on edge of chair, is very pleased with silver tray Norma gives her. As is Maltese custom, she says "thank you" and quickly puts it down behind on the table there, lest the "evil eye" curse takes hold. Johnny is a short but muscular person, full of good humor with a sharp wit, darkly tanned and very thoughtful. Johnny and Paula treat us almost like relatives and kinfolk, and always looking out for us. Paula pulled me out of a dangerous confrontation later on at a picnic where I had separated from the group and was detained by a couple of suspicious persons. She just grabbed my hand, gave everyone a hard glare and pulled me away saying "come on."

Saturday, June 3

    Everyone went to bed shortly after guests left. I slept well with the bed next to the open window where the cool night air was strongest, until the screams of the English baby next door and scolding of Cockney mom woke me up around 6 a.m. I managed to fall back asleep for a while until Edgar, our rental agent, came in to fix the leaky faucet in kitchen below.

    After a short breakfast, Marcia and I drive to Valetta to change some money and open accounts at a bank. Marcia drives. I am not yet trusted on left-hand traffic driving from right hand side of little car where most controls are mounted on the turn signal handle (including the horn!). We park back at Mr. French's garage and walk the rest of the way up the steps and into the grand old city with its narrow streets and crowded sidewalks. Marcia knows the way; we wind up at Taliaferro @ Sons where we try to change money and open accounts, but are directed to offices upstairs. Bank is very busy and full of people running around. Upstairs, we are redirected to offices downstairs. Downstairs again, we are finally connected with a Mr. Azzopardi. There is much confusion over changing Swiss currency and opening accounts. Mr. Azzopardi first agrees, then decides he can't exchange Swiss franc for Maltese pounds. Finally, we get to open accounts with some bank checks from U. S. Then I get directions to a stationary shop where I was able to buy a supply of typewriter paper. After I paid with new Maltese pounds and actually left the store, the clerk rushed out and stopped me, asking to re-examine the change she had given me, apologizing, because everyone was confused about the currency change. We also shop for a camera for me, but prices seem too high and I am disappointed.

Next, Marcia drives us to an open Maltese market: small stalls in large open building. It is rather dark inside, very crowded and full of strong smells. I was not happy there, but managed to follow Marcia around while she made purchase of meat, eggs, vegetables, etc. We return to Marsaxlokk, where lunch was almost ready. Johnny had dropped off some sea urchins, prickly balls you had to crack open. Not my cup of tea, but Norma seemed to enjoy them.

After a lazy afternoon taking care of some details and resting, we three drove south, down to Birzebbuga to the Sea Breeze Restaurant for a nice spaghetti supper, but had to rush back to pick up Johnny and drive to Zabbar for a radio program. The "radio" in Malta was a British re- diffusion type carried by wire directly into homes of listeners.

And Johnny was not just an ordinary person, a gardener by trade at a graveyard up in Vittoriosa; he was a popular Maltese singer-poet performer in a difficult traditional style that Marcia had come to study and on which to write her brilliant doctoral dissertation.

The trip to Zabbar took us North along several back roads past small communities with doorsteps right on the edge of the road and it seemed that the people that lived there took pleasure in sitting in the doorways and sticking their feet into the road. Yes, and it always seemed to me that people there preferred stay in tight groups and clusters, being alone was not a preferred choice.

At the rediffusion, we were ushered quickly into a large studio with a recording booth. Three guitarists were already there in chairs under the mikes. We found seats in the corner with a few other people and the session began almost at once. I noticed Norma and Marcia stealing glances at me seated alongside of them, and smiling a lot as if sharing some great secret. The guitarists started up nicely, in a very pleasant chordal style, with an introduction of sorts. Then Johnny cupped one hand to his ear and started singing. Only it was more like a sustained, tense shout! That was what Marcia and Norma were smiling about. Indeed, there were tears in Marcia's eyes that she wiped away! Maltese folk singers sang in a very unique semi-melodic style, making up a rhyming verse as they sang. The subject could be anything, but usually about politics, love or even a mocking criticism of the other singer. But the strong, dissonant singing style was absolutely unique to this little island. It seems there were three singers, and the one in the middle was a kind of host or commentator, while the other two had at each other. Meanwhile, the contrast between the conventional harmonies of the strumming guitars and the shouting melodies of the singers was painful to a stranger! Later on, when I was used to it, the singing and music did seem very beautiful to me.

The guitars, too, seemed unique. They were made with a crescent-horn jutting out the upper-treble side, projecting downward as it was played. Everything else about them was traditional, the 6 strings, the neck and frets. I played classical guitar in my youth, so I was familiar with the chord fingerings etc., but even though the harmonies they played were the traditional I, IV, V chords, I couldn't recognize the fingerings as they played, and so deduced the strings were tuned differently from classical European models.

We had to leave the studio right after the session ended because something else was scheduled there, so we gathered up Johnny away from his fan club and were directed again through the back-streets (now darkened) to "Aunt Lucy's Bar" in Marsaskala, where everyone had agreed to meet afterwards.

Aunt Lucy's was a long, narrow place with the bar at the far end, with benches and tables along the sides facing each other. We were a bit early, so it took a while for the place to fill up again with the musicians and people from the studio, plus a few others. Resting on the bar itself in one corner I noticed a nice expensive Roberts tape recorder connected to a cassette recorder, already in use. Norma told me that they were already running off copies of this evening's performance for the fans.

Soon the musicians were gathered and guitarists began warming up and starting to play. Johnny and the other singers take turns singing. Several new singers appeared, one of them a new young man with a slightly more lyric style. Joe Fenech, one of the studio singers, sat down beside us and started to translate. Johnny teams up with the new young man and sings to him, "Be careful, if the Americans like you, they will take you back to America with them."

After the singing is done, the bar settles down to drinking. The small friendly man seated to my right buys me a beer; I buy him a beer. Soon I have to use the john. Marcia directs me to go up the stairs in the back and tells me to be careful. Later, she tells me the bar is also a "house" and Lucy is the Madam. Duh! I knew that.

Afterwards, we took off to Paula's parent's house in Querendi. It was Sunday and it was the Saint's day there, and the fireworks were already in progress as we all climbed onto the flat roof. All the roofs are flat, by the way. After a while, sounds of the band starting up in the square below brought us downstairs. The crowd is mixed, but teenagers separate into girl-boy groups. Boys mill about with loose, large gestures, while girls stand, some with folded arms, giggly, short skirts. No body odors. Only small boys shove into people, are tolerated. Band plays well in tune. Everyone is pushed aside as the Catherine wheel firework poles proceed out of the church with the saint's statue and the procession begins amidst booms and strings of fireworks. Afterward, we go into the band house for more beer and food. And that was only the second day in Malta!

Sunday, June 4 - Wednesday, June 21

For me, the following days were taken up with a quest for something to investigate. Marcia and Norma were there for a vacation and to maybe check on some matters pertaining to Marcia's thesis. And to get some new dresses made. I felt the need to take advantage of my situation there and contribute something useful.

Therefore, the following days and weeks were taken up with a search for something I could study and research. I first thought I could find something to do with harmonicas and harmonica players. I could play harmonica and blues harp, an even though I located several music stores in Valetta with harmonica displays (Hohner, always), no one knew of any one there that played a harmonica. One store assistant assured me "is not our instrument."

Norma suggested we look over in the dock and shipping area, that maybe some sailors could be found that played, but even though we nosed around, no one admitted playing or knowing someone who played the harmonica.

At the same time, I went to the magnificent Royal Library in Valetta and located the head librarian, who kindly showed me many ancient texts and early music manuscripts. Bur I couldn't imagine what I could do with them.

Norma made a point of telling me to get my nose out of a library.

Another opportunity opened up when I took the car one day and drove north of Mdina and the magnificent old cathedral there. I was directed to a short, stubby Maltese priest, a younger man, Father Azzopardi. When I introduced myself as an American musicologist and wondering if there was any early music I could see, he looked up at me and intoned: "My son, you are sent to me from God! Follow me!" And he took off down some stairs, past some stacks and went into a room with wooden benches circling in rows. He disappeared for a minute and came back with a large wooden fruit basket, and without further ceremony, he dumped its contents onto one of the tables and explained that they were music manuscripts dating from the early 17th Century and they needed to be catalogued. I was rather amazed and gratified, but I found upon examination that even though they contained music by Monteverdi and other well-known composers of the early 1600's, they were copies of printed score parts. Printed music was very expensive early on, and so churches would purchase one copy and have the parts copied out for the choir and instruments. I was able to visit there every once in a while and do some cataloging for Father but it was a dead end and a thankless task. But I was able later on to do a little bit and then get Father Azzopardi to show me the bells.

Foto 3. Our house "Tokai", Mary at the door, our car out front

Wednesday, June 21

The turning point came on Wednesday the 21st. Mary Grech, our teenage maid, was washing clothes in the bathtub next to my room when I passed by on the way downstairs. She stopped me and asked me if I knew what the church bells had just told her, that someone, not from

Marsaxlokk, had passed away in the hospital. I started to question her closely about that ringing and another, but she seen became annoyed. I think she said "Why don't you go to lunch?" Very Maltese! She said the bells just rang to say things, and to make them happy. I left it at that. Mary is very young and also female, and probably didn't know all that much about the bells. As I learned later on, bell ringing in Malta is the job of boys and men only, like so many other things.

I think it was at this point that I realized what an opportunity this was, and I then resolved to discover and translate for everyone, what it was the bells were saying!

Thursday, June 22

This morning I went out to the Parrish priest's house and had a brief talk with Father Delicata. He met me at the door of his house. It had a yellow door with a gate, identified by Mary Grech, who directed me with care before I left. She told me he was in mourning for his mother, and was concerned about what I was going to ask him. She said talk of bells was OK.

Conversation begins with introductions and establishment of identity. I gave my reasons for calling very briefly. He took me into his office just off to the right of hallway where I met another (local?) priest. They seemed in the middle of some business so I decided to be brief. Second priest offered his hand, which I shook. His hand contact was brief, weak. Father Delicata did not offer, or he had waited for me to offer my hand.

There was the usual conversation establishing purposes, many questions on their part or, rather on part of Father Delicata. That I am here on holiday gives them some relief? Or maybe a pattern they can fit me into, or may bring relief that big American Professor is not swooping down with a lot of questions.

As for the bells, here is some general information first. Father Delicata seemed to think bell ringing developed from Italian customs, although they were slightly different in Malta, as in Spain and South America. The Bells of Birkirkara especially, were spectacular, biggest bells of the Island are found there.

In Marsaxoxx It seems as though the time of day is one of major means of communication, not the pitch or tone of bell. The Angelus bell at 8AM, noon and sunset, is changed for a festal, i.e. rung on a larger bell.

There are 5 bells in Marsaxloxx, not very old. Four of them came from St. Dominic's in Valletta about 25 years ago (c. 1950), when the bells there were replaced with the new ones. The smallest bell was already here. All the bells are named, baptized, and bear Latin inscriptions.

Bells are rung on one tower of the church with ropes leading down to a chamber below. The bells on the other (right-hand) side have to be rung up in the tower. The church has a facade with bell towers on either side. If double strokes are to be used, you have to do it in the tower on the right.

Most interesting: there are some people who hire themselves out to ring the bells at the Saint's feasts. Local people don't like to do it; they want to be out enjoying the feast. "We get people from outside the village, pay them so they will do it right." Feast of Maria Pompey here on the 17th-18th used bell ringers from Zejtun or Zabbar. Think it was Zetun (Zejtun). Will have to ask again. The 2nd Priest said there are groups who know how to ring the bells and who go around to all the festal for hire. Very interesting.

Father Delicata offered to let me look at the bells and take pictures, but later on. He said he would call sometime in the evening. I took my leave then, I didn't want to push too much at first. I thought Father Delicata started to offer his hand. This is going to spook me for a while now, whether or not to shake hands with a priest.

Backup: Initial interest in bells having been aroused, I took the opportunity to ask Father Gaberetti about church bells in Malta Sunday before last when we visited St. Laurence Church in Vittorioso, where he showed us an original Palestrina book of masses. Father Gaberetti seemed to think (he should know?) that the rules for ringing the bells were handed down by the bishop. He mentioned that a rule that no bells should be rung before 6AM was probably ignored and that many places still continued their old ways. This info "cold" from last Sunday (18th) and may be skewed.

Again, it was yesterday (Wed. 21), as I now recall, Mary is washing clothes in the bathroom tub and I am in my room. She calls to me "did you hear the bells? They mean someone in the hospital died." She explains when bells go off at 11:45, it means someone has died in the hospital, or someone not from Marsaxloxx has died. I tried to question her more closely, but she didn't seem to know much more. I am afraid that I annoyed her, because she said (I think) "why don't you go for lunch" (i.e. and leave me alone). I don't think she was angry, just upset. Later on I typed a letter for her. I have been questioning her too closely, and while she is interested in what I am doing, her knowledge is limited.

Norma said bells that signal death ring seven times. Tested this on Mary today and it is correct. Mary asked me what I had found out about the bells when I called on Father Delicata and I was only able to say a few things she had omitted to tell me e.g. that groups of people ring bells for feasts, and last Sunday they were from Zejtun (are they always from Zejtun?)

Friday, 23 June

This evening (23rd) we trip out to St. Thomas Bay to see Hal Tmiem, the "boundary" house we may move into, accompanied by Joan and another Inglese lady. We returned to have drinks with

Inglese neighbors. I couldn't take much and excused myself, especially when I saw Joan was going to tie one on. Had just walked back home, when the doorbell rang and Johnny appeared. He seemed tired and nervous. I hauled him in and slapped a drink in his hand, and we proceeded to have a long conversation, stilted a little at first, but which soon warmed up. Johnny was a little put off (I think) that Norma did not show up to go swimming last Sunday. I explained we thought that if we did not decide to go on this end, we simply would not show up "Maltese time" in Zabbar. He probably didn't understand this, or didn't remember, because he was quite looped Saturday night by the time we had begun to make these arrangements.

Later on, he pulled a wedding invitation out of his shirt, addressed to "Mr. Ottovino and Miss Norma & Marcia." Next Tuesday, his brother is getting married and then, is going to Australia.

Johnny told me a few things about bells. He knew that there were groups of young men that rang them, they were from Zejtun, but he didn't know any of them personally. He told me two stories about the bells in Zabbar. First, his father had helped to mount the extremely large bell they have in that church a number of years ago. He said the Army had come there to help (with a derrick?). The second story was also about this bell, that at one time during Carnival when there were many people in the streets, the huge bell clapper fell off and landed in the only spot in the street where there were no people; a "miraculo!" Johnny also mentioned that the death bells at 11:45 and 12 had to be paid for, that they don't ring for poor people that don't pay. This story lead to a long conversation about the Church and the Malta Labor Party (MLP). He mentioned the story Boissevian recounts (B. the author of an important Malta study), that when the MLP was holding rallies in the different villages, the priests would have all the bells rung to drown the speakers out. When complaints were made, they said they were doing the ringing to bring people to the church, for Jesus. The MLP complained to the English, who slapped a £200 fine on ringing the bells during a political rally. The bells stopped.

Johnny has had many bitter experiences with the church during the strife period some years ago. He said he went for confession once and the priest asked him which party he belonged to. When Johnny said he was Malta Labor Party, the priest asked "why do that thing" and Johnny says "Because I am worker" (lapsing into dialect). Anyway, the priest refused him absolutions, and Johnny got mad and said "OK that's your responsibility; I am going to take communion tomorrow anyway." Typical Maltese: beautiful, and unbeatable. The priest finally gave him absolution and blessed him.

I gather that as the debate grew hotter, even this argument would not avail. Johnny says he learned of a priest in Valletta that would hear confession without asking about politics, and he went to him. After he was blessed, he said to the priest, "I want to ask you one thing," and the priest answered, "I know what it is, do not ask it." Later, the priest was removed from saying mass and hearing confession, and died of a broken heart in two months. Johnny tried another priest after that, but the same political questions came up. Johnny said to the priest, "why you ask those questions, I went to a priest in Valletta, and he don't ask those questions, I went to a priest in Valletta, and he don't ask those things of me," and the priest replied, saying "That priest was a bad man," whereupon Johnny said "I think you are the one, the bad man" and he left. Johnny said he never went to confession for three years after that.

Foto 4. Marsaxloxx Church

Saturday, 24 June

I just returned from a visit to Marsaxloxx church (Foto 4 above) and a long talk and tour with Father Delicata. I put my green outfit on and walked down to the piazza where I spotted Father Delicata just coming out of his door. I waved, and he waited for me to catch up and we talked on the way to the church, just next door. I asked him about getting in touch with the boys from Zejtun who ring the bells on Festal. He said no, he didn't remember their name, but that anyway, they didn't speak English and they had no special knowledge.

He very kindly offered to take me up into the bell tower. He left me at the side entrance and went in back of the altar to get some keys. As he passed the altar, he kneeled or dipped and crossed himself briefly. A small girl in a blue dress came in the door with us, struggling to get a white lace kerchief over her head (it was windy). Having fixed the kerchief, she joined some other small girls who were already occupying the left rear rank of chairs. Seems there were long pews. Father Delicata returned and led me up a long spiral staircase (got a little dizzy and winded) and we came out on the roof, which as strangely humped and bumped. The roof looked like this:

(ex. 1)

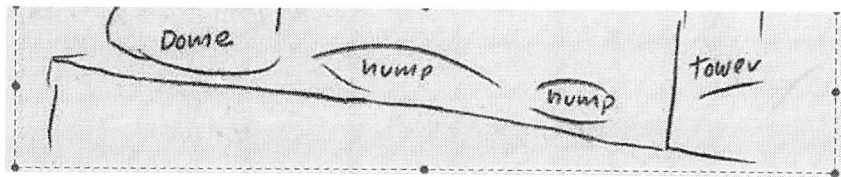

I scrambled immediately to the stage right tower. Father Delicata said to be careful not to be blown with the wind. The stage right tower contained two bells, an immense bell in the center and a smaller one to the front. Father Delicata said that 4 of the bells were made in Malta by a single founder, Guilano, who was the only bell maker in Malta and who died without revealing his secrets to anybody else, and so all bells afterward had to be imported. The right front bell was Italian, "Fonderia + St. Carlo." The rings at the top were different from the others. We could not read the inscription completely here and on the large bell because there was no way to see the other side of the other bell and the inscription on the large bell was too high up. Father Delicata said the large bell was too big for the tower, really, because when it was rung it tended to sway and strike the edge of the other bell and the tower. The edges were indeed worn where this had occurred. I noticed high up in the top of the tower where someone had painted "6/15/67" initials F.O.D? And then "Greech"- this in red paint. Father Delicata thought at first some naughty boys had done it but agreed it could have been from a time when the tower or the bell had been repaired. Noticed some chalked inscriptions, one referred to something- 1972. Another graffiti on the wall, but can't remember.

The stage left bell tower contained three bells, two medium sized and one larger one to the front. The two smaller bells on the side rang while we were there. They are connected to the clock mechanism. The two bells operated by the clock are a major third part in pitch. Father Delicata translated the inscription on the larger, front bell. In effect, "Salmino and Frauggio with clergy and people erect this monument tribute with public and private funds for the church known as Stella Maris," Father Delicata thought this was S. Dominic's now. The bell in this tower in the inside was chipped on the rim facing the other tower. Its date was 1885. I took pictures of the towers and a few of the bay. The layout of the bells:

(ex. 2)

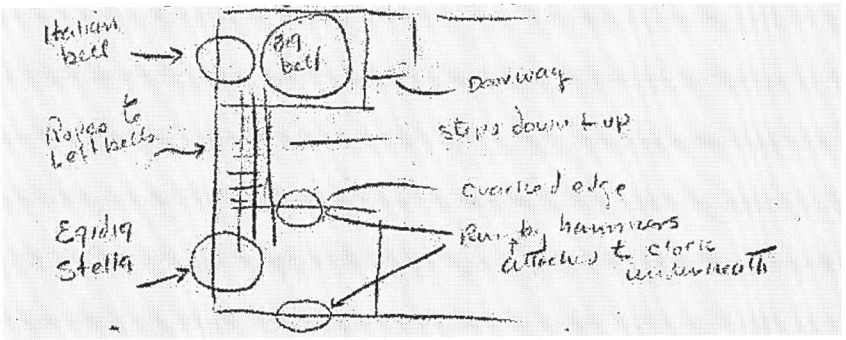

When we returned downstairs, Father Delicata asked if I played the organ. I admitted to some keyboard facility. He led me into the organ stall off the spiral staircase and opened the organ for me. I fiddled with a little Bach first and then improvised some Henry, standing in front. It was larger and better sounding than I expected, and the reverberation in the church was good. The organ had two manuals and a row of stops. Father Delicata said another Father played the organ and one of the Nuns. We closed the roller-top on the organ and descended to the street door. Father Delicata said he had to keep everything locked because of the boys. He told me I could return the next day for the procession, as the Sacristan and some boys who spoke English would be ringing the bells, beginning about 5:45. I thanked him and said I would return.

Earlier, Mary Grec said she would be marching (might be marching) behind a procession to occur about 6:30 tomorrow. She said it was for the Sacred Heart of Jesus. This is an annual affair for dedication in which certain groups rededicate themselves. Later, she said she might not be marching (?!)

Foto 5. Marsaxloxx bells: "Maria" (cracked) above

Foto 6. (Marsaxsloxx bell ringers)

Sunday, 25 June

I arrived at the parish church at 5:30, fully equipped with the Nagra tape deck, microphone, camera and notebook. After negotiating the spiral staircase (counted 102 steps) and pausing for breath, I went out on the roof where I found the Sacristan, a heavy set and balding man balanced on the outer partition, standing unconcerned right on top of the wall, and five little boys, 7-10 years in age. I tried to explain to the Sacristan that Father Delicata had told me I could come and record the bells, but he interrupted and said in quite good English, "Haha, I don't speak English, no no." About that time a young man appeared and sat down near us on the steps, about 18 years old, slender, wide mouth, good smile and slightly long black hair. I learned later his name was Joe Attard. He spoke good English, and I explained through him why I was present. The Sacristan nodded and seemed pleased. He seemed to be a jolly man, very good humored and eager to please. Joe asked if I was a reporter, and I tried to explain why I was there. Don't remember what I said. Have to give my motives some more thought so my explanations will come easier.

The bells were rung twice while I was present. Both times, the additive technique was used, i.e. one bell would start slowly, and the others added one at a time, then most of them would drop out leaving the big bell alone for several strokes. The small boys did all the ringing under the supervision of the Sacristan and Joe. They were having the time of their lives, although the clappers were difficult to manage and the Sacristan and Joe had to help them get started sometimes.

The Sacristan was magnificent, he orchestrated the whole scene directing this bell to begin, this one to slow down, that one to strike harder. It was obvious he was striving to achieve some kind of balance among the bells, and you could tell he was listening very hard.

Of course I was asked to play back the first recording so that all could hear. Forgot about the playback knob on the side and couldn't get the speaker to work, so I let them all have a listen through the earphones. They seemed pleased. After I had put the Nagra back on my shoulder, I waved them together and took a picture of them here on the roof, posed.

I noticed that the roof was "humped" rather in the manner of a fish skeleton, reflecting the shape of the arches underneath.

Joe told me the following. He said that the church here was about 90 years old, that Marsaxloxx used to be part of Zejtun parish, and that Zejtun was the "mother" of Marsaxloxx, and every year gave £50 (at Xmas?). The boys from Zejtun were given £6 for 3AM to 10PM during the festal last weekend. The church at Zejtun (the Sacristan told me this through Joe) has the biggest bell in all Malta. The small, chipped bell on stage left inside is used for the dead only. It was not rung while I was there. Only the 4 other bells were used. The first recording begins with the big bell, the second with the next largest. Something about the order of ringing here, but I didn't get it straightened out. We were interrupted by the necessity of beginning the next salvo.

Joe told me "I think that you are Catholic," but I had to tell him I was Protestant. I was embarrassed. Maybe he was too. I thought the Maltese didn't ask personal questions. Anyway, I couldn't lie to him. But Joe didn't actually ask a question. He made a simple statement. I could have ignored it. I tried to explain how different Malta was, from America and American Catholic churches. Tried to say what was different, i.e. fewer decorations, fewer bells, etc. He said, "more modern, eh?" He also seemed to think that the tradition of bell ringing was Catholic, or common to all Catholic churches. Must check on this. (Something else here, it may come to me).

After the second ringing, the Sacristan straightened out the ropes that had been loosened. Oh yes- the Sacristan said through Joe that the Pater Noster used to be rung at 4AM but the Archbishop stopped it, and restricted the ringing to 6AM.

While we were descending the stairs, I asked Joe if we could meet sometime and talk about the bells. He seemed agreeable, and then suggested we talk outside. But downstairs he led me into the church and gave me a guided tour, I felt very much out of place, as there were people already there, kneeling, praying and fingering rosaries. The walls were hung with pictures over shrines, which became more elaborate the nearer we approached the altar. We passed Father Delicata on the way to the vestry, and I nodded but did not speak. Joe took me past the vestry where about 5 clergy were gathered in various stages of costume. Little choirboys were running around in white blouses. One of them came over to Joe for assistance in fixing the back fastening.

We came out in back of the altar. Joe pointed out the grave of the first parish priest directly behind the altar and inscribed in Latin. It was flush with the floor. I was careful not to step on it but Joe walked right across one edge on our way out. The other side of the church contained a room for storing some of the flags, the pedistal on which the statue was carried and a large case in which various silver chalices and whatnot were stored. I was amazed at the elegance of some of the pieces. Joe said the pedestal was 100 pounds, and I agreed it was heavy: I couldn't move it with my hands. He laughed and said it cost £100. On the walls were framed pictures of various Marsaxloxx processions. Must remember to send Father Delicata some copies of my photos.

Outside we made arrangements to meet this coming Saturday at 1 PM (some confusion about this.) He asked me if I had any Maltese friends, I said I knew Johnny Maniscalco and Carminu Buggeja, and he knew both of these. He gave me his address; 16 Zejtun Road, Marsaxloxx. I should have offered to pick him up or something. Promised to write or leave word if we changed houses.

Then I trundled back towards home; took some pictures of the altar being prepared in front of Our Savior Street; talked briefly to Mary who was holding her nephew, delightful baby of about 3-4 months. Mary said that girls were going to sing.

Returned home to Marcia, Norma and Johnny, Paula and Paulo. Was fed while I reported progress. Norma played back my tape and said the presence was flat. They left for Zurrieq to view fireworks. I finished my meal and scribbled notes. Almost got butter on the Nagra (Norma's expensive Swiss tape recorder). The bells began early, before I had finished eating. Noticed the big bell rang about 30 times- no it was the medium bell, and the big bell came in 1 2, pause, 1 2 3, after which the other bell ended with an emphatic 1 2.

Back on the street, I took pictures of the procession from in front of the Nun's home, "Domus Mariae." Procession order: Nuns with little girls lead by older girl carrying banner. Then clergy with crosses and banners, then little boys, more crosses and clergy, then priests with one under a canopy, then older girls in brown, then older girls still with some women, parents and children. All the women were wearing scarves, then little girls behind scarves and some hats. When the loudspeaker system began about 7:30 with the organ and girl's chorus, the girls and nuns on the porch of the nun's house sang along, some with books. I followed the procession down to the corner and tried to make myself inconspicuous against the wall. I had a very strong sense of belonging with these people as I strolled down the street. The ceremony consisted of a long oration (amplified) by one of the respected intern-like priests, without notes and in Maltese, followed by a Latin prayer. Afterwards, the procession reformed and walked back to the church as the loudspeakers began again with the organ and girl's chorus. There was no singing live down by the altar, but I recorded some people singing with the music as they strolled past. I think I caught the words "Maria Pompey." I left as the procession passed St. Pius V Street feeling very much like a character coming off a movie set.

Monday, June 26

In the morning, I go early to Mdina. Father John Azzopardi has finished sorting the Mss (manuscripts) and gives me copies of shelf list. We go upstairs to see Medieval Mss in display cases, find five magnificent choir books and two XI century books with heightened neumes. Later, I ask to see the printed music, discover there are five shelves of uncatalogued 17th century part books. We pull one shelf and start sorting. First book I open is Monteverdi's Sevla Morale. Sorting seems to indicate Mss are copies of existing printed works in collection. Father Azzopardi disappointed. Says he will continue to sort part books and make list; wants me to help him decide the titles later.

Tuesday, June 27

Tuesday evening: To the wedding of Johnny's brother at Zabbar. We are late (again, don't know why they put up with it. Norma insists on driving and we are lost. Anyway, we left late.) Mary Abbar (Paula's sister) is waiting for us on the corner in her yellow dress. We have to go around the church to find a parking place and make another wrong turn. We finally pull up in front of what we discover later is the reception hall. Mary is a little scolding. As we enter the church the mass is almost over. Bride and groom are kneeling in front of altar, people returning from taking sacrament. Most people are kneeling. We sit a little in back with Mary. Marcia has a scarf; Norma brazens through without a scarf. Mary uses a handkerchief. Church is usual: canopy over altar, six candles, unlit, with six smaller candles below, they are lighted. Priest accompanied by layman. Seems very perfunctory not as much effort or class as it might have been. Notice that hanging lights like crowns consists of circular neon lights; strange in those surroundings. The service concludes soon after we are seated, about 10 minutes. The bride and groom get up. Everyone rises. Some delay at the altar, I couldn't' see what. Photographer, tall skinny man hung with light meters and dripping film wrappings in isle, takes pictures as they come up isle. Johnny and his brothers are very handsome in dark suits. Bride is very young, semi dark complexion, slender, very delicate features. Johnny's brother is swarthy, handsome, wavy black hair with long sideburns.

Earlier, Marcia had bought a card. Marcia and Norma decided to make a present of American dollars, since the bride and groom would be going to Australia and couldn't take much with them. I believe some relative on Paula's side was going to get him a job as a stevedore.

More pictures taken at the church door, then down to the rented, black shiny car. Photographer takes picture of couple in car. They drive off in style, even though the reception is just around the corner. We go with family to reception hall, downstairs. It is a long rectangular room with banks of folding chairs, movie theatre style, set in rows along one side. There is a long bar on the other side, piled with goodies. A band consisting of two electric guitars, an electric organ, an accordion and a snare drum set, is stationed at the far end of the room, near the steps. Notice a young girl in blue (short) pants suit sitting nearby. We are taken to set of chairs near the stage at the opposite end of the hall. Soon, the band strikes up and the bride and groom enter to the music. People rise to form reception line. There are six people on the stage, the parents of the bride, the bride and groom, and the parents of the groom. It is a little crowded. We go up and shake hands. Norma gives the envelope with the card and money to me to give to the groom. As we peel off from the reception line, we are given a plate of ice cream with a biscuit.

Diagram of room:

(ex. 3)

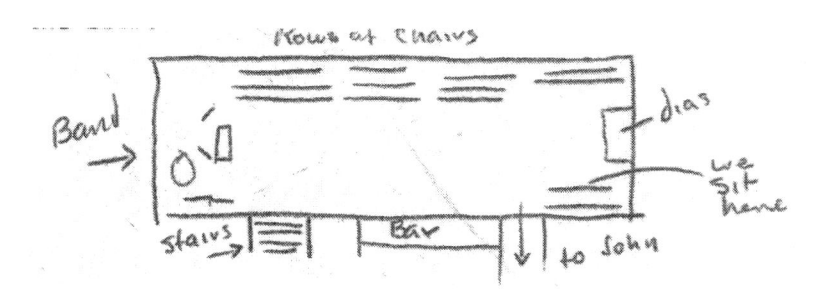

After the congratulations are complete, the photographer asks the couple to come down for the dancing picture. The poor dears shuffle very self-consciously- they do not know how to dance at all. Johnny's brother (smiles,- keeps calling me Joe) says it is to start the dancing. Bride is exhausted, pained by uncomfortable headdress, which she keeps trying to adjust. She is close to tears. The couple disappears upstairs and the dancing begins. The following is out of order, but I notice an older couple jitterbugging. Later, the young set twists. All dances very old, not so well executed, but they are trying and having a good time. Clothing styles very mixed; suits to flashy bell bottoms for men, long below-the-knee dresses of heavy material to miniskirts for the women. Some young girls with eye make-up (very effective), some only with lipstick and painted nails. Some young men also conservatively dressed. Disparity reflects what? Urban-rural, social status? Wealth? I have seen very modern dress on girls sitting on their doorsteps in poorer parts of town. Probably education, exposure to European and American styles.

We are taken upstairs by the family, to an auditorium and stage where the bride and groom are posing against backdrop for more pictures with family and friends. Marcia, Norma and I are photographed, and return to ballroom.

After mass, the whole structure is dominated at first by the photographer, just as signing is influenced by tape recorders. Learn later that there is an option between "portrait" and "album" style of photographs; the album style being the one selected for this wedding.

In the ballroom, more goodies (sweets) foisted up on us by the caterers ("King's Own Caterers, Valletta"). Drinks: Scotch and Vermouth in small glasses. I take Vermouth and later wish I hadn't. Smiley takes me up to bar for brandy and Schweppes. Later, Johnny does the same and I switch to beer. I bring Norma one because she is being inundated. Sandwiches and "savories" arrive, food and drink being spilled or discarded, floor getting slippery.

The band plays intermittently and the dancing continues. As the evening grows older, they seem to drop the pseudo- European dances, (waltzes, ballads), and there is more rock- and more folk-oriented music which results in more active participation. The young girl in blue pants is the vocalist, has a very deep penetrating voice for one so young. She sounds like some old woman with a whisky alto. I notice her tummy is slightly protuberant, Norma bets she's pregnant.

(Comment on earlier query): Norma says difference in dress among young girls of same age is due to whether or not they are married, which makes sense. Marriage is so permanent that it must make a profound difference in life styles, especially in almost-Arabic- purdah places. Separation between sexes is so complete that one wonders how they manage to marry at all. Probably functions to hold population down.

Observation: (along same lines) tendency for females to dance with females, males with males. Children also grouped along same lines. Again, I see many pairs of girls. One pair of sisters is dressed alike in miniskirts. Male groups are less homogeneous. Girls in pairs provide protection, respectability; i.e., not seen talking to men alone. Close intimate friendships developed among girls, sharing secrets, helping with assignations?

Another highlight comes with cutting of the cake. Photos are taken again, much applause. Drinks begin to flow freely. I did not notice that the cake was actually sliced up and passed out. Impression is that knife inserted for single cut and left in cake. Noticed woman removed small angel-like figure hanging over top of cake: symbolic or accidental? Must ask.

The food kept coming. Definite turnover when it is stopped being served and caterers begin to collect dishes and bottles. Drinks constantly available at bar. Floor is getting more and more slippery. It is marble in the first place. Sciclunas pre-empt dance floor near the bandstand. Norma is whisked out on dance floor and performs with grace and style. Brothers becoming more affectionate as they get more zonked. I am getting zonked, too. Round dances start. Norma and Paula get Johnny between them in circle dance. Johnny enjoying himself, dancing with raised arm and thumb. I am hauled out into a circle dance by Paula. Everyone keeps slipping on floor, especially Johnny's father who is holding onto my right hand. My middle finger is sore the next day. Dance solo with Mary, who has been after me all night to dance with her.

Final highlight: Johnny asks me "when I told you, you come help me." Shortly thereafter, he beckons me and we go along with friends and brothers to the dressing room just off the corridor to the toilets. Smiley is always volatile and prankishly hammers on the door until half of it is opened (it is one of those double affairs). The bride has already changed into blue street dress, the type called "midi," and she is wearing a blue hat with a brim. The people rush in. Smiley just about tears the other door down getting it open. I am somewhat puzzled, but it is obvious that something of an emotional nature is going to happen. The groom is dragged out into the corridor and it is obvious they are going to carry him into the ballroom on the shoulders. In fact, this is probably why Johnny wanted me to help. The groom seems to resist then goes limp. I hoist him up, the Johnny tells me "leave it" and they carry him out, crying and limp. The bride is also hoisted up (by Smiley and others- felt I shouldn't lay hands on since I was asked to lay off and since it became clear that the family was becoming involved in and emotional leave-taking).

The bride and groom were carried protesting and weeping out into the ballroom by a crowd of weeping, slipping people, brought together and all are embraced and have a good cry. Everyone becomes very emotional, yes, well, there's no other way to say it. I never saw such a crowd of happy-sad people. Afterward, the bride and groom escape back into the dressing room to recover. People started to leave. I embraced Johnny's only single brother (he will probably marry the attractive little black headed girl he is always with, since they are always together, one can presume they are engaged). Some kind of argument followed, but I didn't catch the circumstances. The groom came out and I shook his hand and embraced him. The father came up – now well into his cups- and hugged me and kissed me. He did the same to Norma, and then I got a repeat performance.

Upstairs, the bride and groom left in their hired car. We left immediately afterward, having been fortunate in our chance selection of a parking place right in front of the hall. What a party.

Wednesday, June 28

Imnaria day. Johnny dropped by in the morning. He had made arrangements to film something for the TV with Surgent and asked us to come. We agreed to meet him in Zabbar at 3:45 Maltese time (we are always late and have had to excuse ourselves time after time by explaining that "American time" is different- always later). Almost late again as we discover we have no 7" empty tape reels. We had to unwind two full reels into baskets. We finally assemble all the recording equipment and scurry off to Zabbar. I drive this time. At Johnny's house, I went in to get the family while Marcia and Norma stay in the car with all the stuff. Norma had been rewinding the tapes on the way over in the back seat. No use, all of us have to be brought in for a beer. Johnny had rented a car for the day. Thought we were to meet his brother there, but he didn't show up and we left in two cars. In Johnny's car were Johnny, Paula, Mary and little Paul.

Johnny drives like a demon. Marcia was elected to follow, no contest. She drives very well. We drove (flew) to an intersection outside of Mdina to wait for Surgent, who appeared shortly. Then we waited for the TV van, which appeared shortly (again) and then for the third party who arrived with family in an ancient black car. I bought an extra roll of film at a tourist shop- the intersection was just outside the remains of a Roman villa. We had followed parts of a viaduct on the way over.

The caravan assembled and we went westward to a hamlet called Ballija- perched on some hills and hardly obvious as a settlement at all. We had difficulty in parking on the slopes and narrow roads. The filming took place at an inconspicuous bar, identified by a

Coca-Cola sign and a hand-lettered sign. The bar was located down a driveway and the entrance was sunken and surrounded by a small flower garden. Surgent brought out some costumes and he, Johnny and the other man put on sashes, vests and hats. Surgent changed into a peasant shirt. The tall tanned playboy from our earlier visit to the TV was there, with a small cameraman and another person.

The shooting was "on location", color for the singing we had witnessed earlier, the mini-opera Surgent had concocted (or the producer had concocted, the one with the small girl "Rita", singing "anneli wahudah", in a head scarf and long dress).

Foto 7. (B&W) TV singers: Rita, Surgent, ?, and Johnny

One of her girl friends was also present and watched the proceedings with us. She and Rita both had very striking blue-gray eyes.

The small man with the camera, city-dressed with steel rimmed glasses and slightly long hair began to talk to me in Maltese. When I replied in English he said "Oh, sorry," and began to question me. I had dressed in jeans and blue shirt, very informal, with red suspenders. The usual line followed: very surprised to see an American here. Did I understand what was going on, could I stand the singing, what was I doing in this God-forsaken place etc. etc.?

The filming consisted of several takes and retakes of Johnny walking down to greet Surgent, Rita, and the other man. Rita was invariably sent inside to fetch wine. I took several photos, but later discovered the ASA on my camera was set too low: the film may not come out. During one break, cokes were fetched and the small cameraman handed me a crisp biscuit to sample, and came over once again to give me a bite of feta-like cheese. I shared my biscuit – or whatever, it was like hard Armenian bread- with a small grey cat that gobbled the tough crumbs.

Noticed several mint like odors, the cactus patch off to one side was pleasantly smelly although covered with spiders and spider webs. The Small Camera Man said the Spaniards had brought them over.

Afterward we went back to the car, which had been parked precariously on the shoulder of a hill. Marcia backed it out with Johnny's help. We got in and dove down to where Johnny had parked his car near a barn or something. Then something very unfortunate occurred that colored the rest of the day somewhat- at least for me. A small cat had sat down in the back of the right rear wheel, and Johnny didn't see it and he backed over it several times before it lay still. He got out and apologetically flipped the body over into the field by the tail. Marcia grumbled about putting her down for some more work on killing cats, because she had really yelled at Johnny and swore. My stomach was off for quite a while.

We drove back to Mdina and were routed around the walls by the police. We arrived at the Buskett and Verdala palace shortly thereafter and found some parking places back of the road without any trouble. Johnny apologized for the cat, but said he couldn't help it. Marcia agreed the cat too "wanted it" since it was too dumb to move. We slung the tape recorders and the other gear and made off up the road to the entrance to the Buskett, which is the only extensive collection of trees in Malta. It is situated along two sides of a valley underneath a large, square palace built for the Inquisition. The trees are stunted pine-cedar trees growing on rocky soil. The descent to the fairgrounds is made down a narrow, shaded road. Johnny carried Norma's TR and Mary carried my briefcase. We stopped to look at the agricultural exhibit. True to Father Gabrietta's prediction, almost all the first prizes went to "Attard-Zebbug." There were ducks, turkeys, doves etc. and all manner of produce. Up from the shed containing the exhibit, on the same mall, there was a bandstand being prepared for the singing contest. Johnny took us up the hill to a restaurant and insisted on pouring some more beer down us. Norma wanted to go to a toilet, but the one there wasn't working. Norma and Marcia had been meeting many people they had known several years ago. Aunt Lucy and Cetta were there.

We went back down and staked out a place in back of the bandstand. Norma disappeared with Mary to find a john. The place was not very crowded when we arrived (about 6) but the crowd soon began to come in.

(ex. 4)

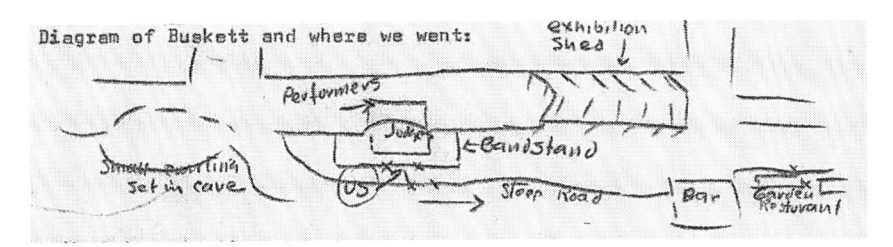

Foto 8. Buskette

L to R: Macia, Joe Fenick, Johnny, Paula, Paulo, Mary Abbar (Paula's sister)

    We sat protecting our places for a long time. Marcia went ambling with her note book. I settled myself back against a tree with my feet over the edge of the wall, feeling very snug and watching the people. Johnny handed me two sandwiches with oil and tomato paste- greasy, but good. I got gunk all over my pipe and camera, and a big stain on Marcia's tape recorder, which did wipe off. After all. Norma and Mary came back with drinks. People kept piling in on the ledge where we sat. Two large females situated themselves on either side of Norma. Only time I've seen Maltese get pushy. Mary came and set next to me on the wall. Paul was next to her and then Paula. Later, Mr. Fenech, the (troche) singer I had met at Lucy's bar, came to join us. We had seen him earlier? No, I think he walked up as we were getting settled and then came later to sit with us.

The balcony of the bandstand below us was fenced off for the judges. The platform for the singers had been erected in front of this and four microphones were already in place. After a considerable period of waiting, all the judges and technicians assembled. Surgent was dancing back and forth across the stone railing, busily playing the impresario. A long series of song duels followed, with interludes consisting of people climbing back and forth across the stone railing. Each set of duelists was introduced by a man, seated at a table just in back of the performers. We decided not to make any recordings after all, because the sound was so bad and we could barely hear the guitars at all.

Notable among the performers were:

1. Bambinu singing with Chedda. Many of the performances centered on wit and funny remarks tinged, I suppose, with references to sex.
2. Johnny Navaro- small skinny man with huge woman, decked out in Pseudo-peasant costume, S. Italian style. Vaudeville mannerisms and slap stick routines. Crowd seemed very pleased and very amused at the performance. Johnny Navaro's arrival caused considerable stir among the crowd. Later, he doffed his costume and assumed a shirt with bow tie and went back to speak to judges.
3. Joe Fenech's fatt: Joe slipped down off the wall and performed this special type of song which I gather is a type of ballad. It was rather long but well received. Afterward, he promised Marcia he would give her the words.
4. Old woman standing among crowd in bandstand begins to sing. Mary says to me "Chou Makkok" i.e. "goodbye monkey" i.e., clever one. She was behaving in an eccentric manner,

laughing at her own lyrics. Once she took a 7-Up bottle and waved it about in front of her crotch, spilling liquid in imitation of a phallus. Some people drew back in distaste when she started this.

Finally, at Johnny's suggestion, we extracted ourselves from the crowd at the ledge and proceeded through the crowd back up the road to the bar and garden where we had gone for drinks before. We passed a crowd of people packed tightly around a group of singers. Marcia had said before, that the serous singing went on back up in the hills, and that the contest was strictly for amateurs and entrepreneurs. We passed through the bar and found a table near the open place that served as a kitchen. One man in a blood stained apron was busily killing rabbits and butchering them, which did not stimulate my appetite much. The rabbits were dissected and popped into the skillets nearby. Another person was dipping dishes in water and wiping them. The garden was crowded and noisy. There were about four rows of narrow tables and chairs, he tables covered with white tablecloths that were covered with stains and crumbs by now. A waiter brought two bottles of wine. Johnny made the order for fried rabbit, and two plates of bread were placed on the table.

While we were waiting for the food to arrive, Joe Fenech and two of his friends came up. I thought I saw some pained expressions on Johnny's and Paula's faces. They stood and talked for a long time. One of Joe's friends had been a building superintendent in New York and had retired and had come back to Malta to live. He said he could live very well in Malta on his retirement, but that it was impossible to do so in New York. He was a bachelor and had purchased a house, sight unseen, In Sliema, I believe. Of course, any Maltese is fortunate to find a house at all.

The rabbit began to arrive, and Joe and Company seated themselves at the end of our table to wait for their own order. Paula dished out the rabbit in generous portions (as usual). I was off my feed, because the rabbit slaughter 30 feet away reminded me of the unfortunate cat of the afternoon. I think it brought home to me how real death is to our lives, and how well it is carefully hidden from us in our cities and suburbs. How thin is the veneer of civilization etc. and how much closer are the peasants and country people to reality, to pain and to passion. Maybe it is better, in a way, to have these realizations, than to be protected from them by the veil of sophistication and urbanization. Death is real, people fornicate and kill each other, perform kindnesses, acts of love and acts of passion. How complicated are the motivations of so-called educated people, and yet the results are similar, only they are dressed up in fancy thoughts and sophisticated reasoning.

Anyway, my stomach was off. I managed to hack some of the rabbit into bite-sized pieces with my pocketknife (which Norma had lent me in New Orleans in anticipation of such an event) and choke some of the meat down. Actually, it wasn't very well done. I cut it up and left most of it on my plate, giving the liver and kidneys to Norma. The wine was good and I had several glasses. Johnny and his family ate with gusto. Johnny insisted on sharing a bottle of wine with Joe Fenech and his friends and afterward distributed the remainder. He also got a bottle of 7-Up which he poured into the wine glasses.

Earlier I had asked Norma if there was any way to prevent Johnny from paying for the meal and Norma said there was no way in the world. When we left we would just have to calculate and buy some suitable presents. We must be into Johnny about £20-30 by now.

After the meal we loaded up again and made our way slowly out carrying our equipment. Norma paused to talk with Joe Fenech and friends, who said their fond farewells, and to speak to several other friends. Everyone else had gone down the road a little further and had also stopped to talk with some people. We extracted ourselves at length and threaded our way down the hill and past the bandstand on the right and then went into the road leading back up the hill to the exit. I was accosted by two young men. They wanted me to take their photos. I explained I was carrying a tape recorder, whereupon they wanted to sing for me. Everyone else had gone on ahead. They asked if I was Swedish, and I said I was American. They offered me a bottle, and I refused at first, but decided what the hell and took a good swig (after examining the label). About that time someone took my hand and drug me off. It was Paula, saying "come, trouble." Timely succor. Some of Johnny's protectionism extended through the distaff side?

We caught up with the rest. Johnny paused at several busses parked on the side of the road selling various goodies, but didn't buy anything. I had noticed several cream colored busses with loads of tourists forging their way through the crowd and disgorging fair haired Inglese or whatever. All foreigners are classed as Inglese first. Once a smaller van insisted on pushing its way through the crowd on the road which made way for it as best as it could do. As the bus passed, the young people struck up a chorus of the Dies Irae, of all things.

Soon we passed up the hill on the other side. The fairgrounds occupy a small narrow valley, I saw, and the crowd thinned out. Progress up the hill was slow, as we were tired and the hour was late, or relatively so. It was about 1 AM. Johnny had to work at 6:30 the next morning, or rather this same morning. I noticed many families settled under the trees (low stunted pine trees growing seemingly out of the rough limestone ledges) to spend the night, as was customary. Cars kept going up and down the narrow road. Once we encountered a group of people around a card player who was taking bets against the probability of two cards he would throw down and then turn over. Johnny said that you would win at first and then get taken.

Back at the parking place, we discovered we could just get out if we lifted one car slightly out into the road, which we proceeded to do. Marcia squeezed out into the road and waited until we directed Johnny out- he was parked in a small space directly behind us. But a honky bus came up just then and Marcia took off. We got Johnny's car out and he loaded us all inside and took us down the road. Norma and I wondered what Marcia would do now, but decided she would wait, rather than try to circle back around to pick us up. We found Marcia waiting for us at the next intersection and we transferred. Johnny then took the lead and led us a merry chase to Dignli and Siggiewi, having been forced away from a more reasonable route by the green-clad police. Incidentally, the police wear no guns or carry no clubs. Once we stopped at a crossroad and Johnny sought directions from a motorbike driver and his wife, who circled back a ways to view a road sign and then lead us down a very narrow road. I noticed a plastic piping of some kind laid down next to the left hand rubble wall. Eventually we came out on the road to Qormi and left Johnny and family at the turn-off to Luqa, after waving goodbye.

Thursday, June 29

Recuperation day. Marcia, Norma and I finally decide to leave Marsaxloxx for Hal Tmiem because 1), the English Col. who owns Tokai is soaking us too much rent and now he wants even more. 2) Hal Tmiem is free, a palatial farm belonging to a rich psychiatrist who went to England for an operation. One of Norma's friends had cabled, asking permission for us to move in. Real motive: Marcia and Norma want to coddle the damn cat that lived there. Honestly!

Marcia finally tells Mary we are leaving- about time. I insisted we give her an extra week's pay. Mary, unperturbed, says she still has the other job in the afternoon with the Inglesi. The next day, I found out that actually, the Ingliesi had already left, so Mary really had no job. Is Mary too young to react in front of older people, in front of Inglesi? Never saw her react very much to anything, except in very understated terms. The day she came in after nearly electrocuting herself washing the floors too near the electric wall plug, she seemed very brisk and mad. I even thought she was mad at me. When Mary left for the day, I gave her the small key chain with the harmonica on it that I had been saving for her. She had been very interested in my harmonica playing, but was too shy to let me show her anything about it.

Thursday is Mnaria, a holiday and therefore no mail. On a stroll down Quay Street at 5 PM, I noticed only MLP and Felix bar are open. Felix and MLP just two doors away and thus may have affiliated opinions. Opening the bars may have been for display purposes.

Returning, I meet one of the girls who had been with Mary's sister at the festal. I learn she is Johnny M's sister, and I recognized the similarity in complexion, hair and build. Last Sunday, during the procession, I noticed her and Mary's sister clothed in matching pants suits. No, not during the procession, when was it?

Norma and Marcia with Johnny M. go to Valletta to see "Taming of the Shrew." Johnny M. very interested in acting, would like to be an actor, but lacks education and opportunity, working in his father's boat house on St. Pius V Street. He is remarkable perceptive and mature for his years.

It is very hot, so I go down to quay where the breeze is, about 9:30. Sure enough, the Grech sisters appear, arm in arm, all dressed up. Strange inversion where you wear old clothes to work and dress up when you're off work- just the opposite with me. I learn Mary's sister's name is Lena (we were never introduced). She is about 22, unmarried, doesn't like bells or small children, according to her accounts of working for the Inglesi near the church. The Grech brother works as a gardener doesn't speak English but could understand the Arabic of his employer. Lena is a very inquisitive girl, dark and good-looking, but loud with large gestures. She wonders why I went to see the priest; did I want to change my life? The way she put it was typically Maltese "I think you want to change your life"- not a direct question, in other words. Was I a Christian? I tried to explain Protestantism, but neither had any concept of what I was talking about. Lena did most of the talking; Mary was silent as is usual when the sister is around. One can see she is very dependent on Lena and very much influenced by her. Most of the time Mary stood with her arms in back of her, looking at Lena. I tried to catch her eye, but she wasn't playing. They seemed relieved when they learned I had been baptized. Lena says bells are rung at 4 AM, but only on Sunday.

Finally, Lena says "immorru" (the Maltese way of saying "we're going to go and you can't stop us) and they leave. It is here that I began to catch another characteristic of the Maltese, the fact that they don't dawdle with elaborate goodbyes. They just say "I am going" and they leave. There's no stopping them politely after that. Mary had always announced her departures in the same way.

Friday, June 30

Moving day; very hot, almost no breeze moving. We take most of the stuff to Hal-Tmiem, our new home, which is very hot and full of bugs. I return to Marsaxloxx early for my appointment with Joe Attard. Mary is piddling about, washing linens. I had promised to help her move the beds back to where they were before. I went to Tony's bar and got some drinks for the interview, and gathered as much of the remaining stuff together (mostly bottles) and packed it in the car.

Waiting for Joe, I had another talk with Mary. I learned that two brothers and one sister are born dark. She then went on to ask about the blacks in America. Don't suppose there is any connection. Mary herself has a fair complexion, tanned from the sun. Her knees are red from scrubbing and her poor hand and fingers are bleached and swollen. Lena had a steady boyfriend, but wouldn't marry him, preferring to wait for someone she really loved. She is 22 years old, late for marriage as I gather. Mary's father worked for the RAF. Some Italian was coming to see her, asked her to walk with him, but she didn't like him and didn't intend to go. She likes to walk, once went hiking from Rabat. She is saving money for a dowry.

I just noticed that two Italian sea men were fined for illegal entry into Marsaxloxx on July 2, having rowed ashore from a visiting motor yacht; this information from Malta Times, July 4th. Any connection? Was this Mary's boyfriend?

Mary interests me because after all one reads about the highly moral character of the Maltese, she is a sixteen year old girl asking personal questions and flirting with an older man, talking with the boys in the street and admitting to foreign boyfriends, one, an English boy, Diggy Boyd, who left when they threw the RAF out, and now an Italian. Mary and Lena would make good studies of the outsiders. They love Inglesi and hate their surroundings. How typical is this today in Malta?

Joe Attard arrives promptly at 1. Mary leaves and we go up to sit on the roof at Joe's request. I was unsuccessful at cramming a cold drink down his throat. He said he had had a drink at home. I was much taken aback, because this behavior in a Maltese seems to indicate they don't want any favors from you. Joe was able to tell me some things about the bells. I am going to incorporate this material later in a summary. I was surprised to learn that Joe didn't know what the clock patterns meant he said he preferred his watch. Mary did not know either. My own notes were so intermittent that I did not catch the patterns, but I was sure they were present. Joe wrote down some questions to ask the sexton. We agreed to meet on Monday. There was some confusion as I tried to explain that we were moving from Marsaxloxx and I would meet him at Tony's bar at 4 PM. I think he thought I didn't want to meet him in my home.

Having moved everything to Hal-Tmiem finally, we decide to have supper out at the Sea Breeze Restaurant in B'buga, which means spaghetti, since everything else is too tough to chew(!) We returned to Marsaxloxx to spend the night. I go out to get a paper at Tony's and encounter – you guessed it- the sisters Grech. Follows here a strange encounter: Lena asks "are you drunk?" and I say no, are you?; a little taken aback. Then she says it must be the beard, excuses herself, says she is not herself tonight. I gathered I had some body odor, which can smell like whisky on a Caucasoid. I suggested it might have been the pipe I was smoking. We left abruptly. I passed them sitting on the quay, but only said "goodnight." The next day, Mary semi-apologetically explained her sister was acting silly. I suppose I do smell after a hard day's work of shifting boxes about, but the Maltese have positively no body odor at all to my weak schnozzle, muted as it is by perpetual Pennsylvania sinus. I am rather insulted and resolve to sweat less for the Maltese.

Saturday, July 1

Here, a vague day; much rearrangement of furniture, gathering of foodstuffs, & swatting of flies. Hal-Tmiem is filthy and there is no sign of the maid.

Back up for several tidbits I should have mentioned earlier:

1). I don't remember if it was Friday or Saturday, but I dropped into the MLP bar and had a soda. Three people were present, a young man with long hair and side burns, an older woman and one customer besides me. The young man and the older woman were behind the small bar. The walls had pictures of Mintoff, the Prime Minister, and several other political notables. Over a side door hung two lobster or crab claws tied together with what looked like Xmas tinsel and hung after the manner of horns. Over in the far right hand corner was a small shelf with a religious statue and a candle burning in a white glass with a cross painted on it. I noticed later that Tony's bar, the one closest to the church, had a large religious picture and brick-a-brat with candle prominently or strategically located exactly in the center over the bar. The MLP bar was also hung with fishing net and some other fishing tools.

2). Mary Grec is very anxious about Edger S., whose "flat" we were staying at in Marsaxloxx. He is kind of major-dromo manager for foreign landlords, veddy English, in fact half English. Mary is very frightened of him and perhaps uneasy she will have to work with him in the house for a day or so, picking up after us. She seemed to take offense at something I said about E.S. – can't remember what. She said "you say that because you are a man, but you don't know what kind of man he is. Please, you won't tell?" What is going on? Is E.S. a dirty old man? Mary had said several weeks ago "he likes too much, the girls." Has he accosted her, and she has to put up with it because of E.S.'s influence as contractor of maids for Inglesi flats? I could see the fear in her eyes.

Saturday continued: we decide to case Lucy's bar, as Chedda had said she might be singing there. Norma decides to drive again, an unperturbed experimenter and explorer of Maltese roads; she takes us the longest route imaginable, through Marsaskala. Lucy's bar is actually called the "Lucky Bar." It is situated off a side street on the road running down by the "Freedom Press" in Marsacala. The place was jammed packed as we arrived, and a large group of people were blocking the entrance. We could hear singing, and identified Ragel and some others. Marcia theorized that the big-wigs had gotten together for some serious singing. We tried to slip through Aunt Lucy's parlor to get into the back of the bar with the tape recorder, but they wouldn't let us. The bar is a house for prostitution, and all the girls were sitting around inside, mostly older women, large and lumpy. We waited around for a while, hoping the music would end and the crowd clear out, but it went on and on. The bars were obliged by law to stop all singing at 11, The police regard the signers as a bunch of troublemakers because fighting used to break out a lot. And, as it was nearing 10:30, Marcia and Norma debated as to what other bars might be doing business. The option went to Zejtun and we checked the three singing bars there, but all was quiet. Marcia suggested the other singers might be singing in back of the church at Hamrun since there might be some custom involved with the festal in progress there on this night. But it was too late, and we returned to Hal-Tmiem.

Sunday, July 2

A very indistinct day. I had sat up late the evening before typing my notes and had gone to bed about 1 AM and tried to sleep without success. It was very hot, buggy and dirty. The move had unsettled me, I think. I always have trouble adjusting to a new location. About 4 AM I gave up and went up to the roof with a bottle of gin. I remember watching the sun come up and the peasants going out to work. Personal crisis began to make trouble, I suppose, in my mind. Anyway, I finally turned in on a cot on the roof, to be partially awakened by Johnny's voice down stairs – something about going somewhere with him because his brother – something. I think Norma got me down stairs and I got dressed or was dressed. Don't remember much about the drive out or the drive back. However, the situation as best I can recall is this: Johnny's brother, the one whose wedding we attended and who is leaving soon for Australia, won several trophy cups at a shooting match. We were taken to Johnny's brother's mother's farm, the brother here is the dapper one (the one

I call "Smiley"). On second thought I think it is his wife's mother's farm. Anyway, it is not far away from Hal-Tmiem. We sat around in a large square room. Present, as far as I can remember, were Johnny, Smiley (the groom), the elder Scicluna, Smiley's wife, the Bride, - quite a different person in her plain dress now, and barefooted, but still quite lovely – Johnny's sister. Paula might have been there.

The loving cup was filled with Scotch and passed around, which didn't do anything for my state of sobriety. The winning shotgun was shown to me, a small, light automatic, think they said it was 12-gauge, and if so, it must pack quite a whollop.

I don't remember returning at all. Evidently I was poured into bed, and when I regained consciousness, it was suppertime. Johnny, Paula and little Paul were there and we had a pot- luck dinner together.

Monday, July 3

Marcia and I go to Sliema and Valetta for supplies. I met Joe Attard at Tony's. He wanted to go to the house, - maybe there is something wrong with Tony's for this, for meeting in a bar? I drove Joe home and got him to take a beer. He had seen the sextant and gave me much information on the bells. He had brought a paper he had done on the history of Marsaxloxx, which I will peruse, condense and return to him on Thursday at 4.

Joe began to ask some personal questions about Marcia and Norma and myself. Norma had come in briefly and I introduced her. What upset me most may be only a gap in understanding, but it seems to me he asked about my university, then about writing me, wanting my address. He speaks a little indistinctly so it is hard to understand through the accent of his school English. It is possible he was making a homosexual pitch, trying to tell me something, because he said he didn't want to make trouble, was I married, etc. I guess I acted flustered, because he dropped it. What gives?

That evening I went to Marsaxloxx for a walk and a newspaper. The Grech sisters appear on the balcony. After a brief conversation I tried announcing I was going. It seemed to make a satisfactory conclusion. Who is supposed to say this? What situation, what advantage to the one who makes up his mind to leave first? What are the limits of politeness here?

Tuesday, July 4th

To Mdina to help catalogue printed music at the cathedral museum with Father Azzopardi. He is very friendly. The bells there are different form Marsaxloxx and more sonorous. Father Azzopardi seems pleased I am interested in the bells, says many people are trying to stop them. He thinks they are harmonious. He says sometime he will take me for lunch and we can go up and look at the bells. He said one of the bells dates from 1565. Later, I return to Hal-Tmiem and then solo to B'buga via uncertain route for 4th of July lunch. In the afternoon, I write letters and sleep.

Backup: Either Friday 30th or Saturday 1st, Norma sent me to the small bar down the street to get a case of Hopleaf beer. I entered through some hanging strips of plastic that served as a door. It was almost night. As I went up the street I passed a parked car and a boy and rather heavyset young girl, talking to the driver. I think it was the same girl we had spoken to the week before when Moria, Norma's Inglese friend had gone with us to show us Hal-Tmiem. The girl was sitting with some older people on a stone bench across from the bar. The girl waved and said hello in a very loud, deep voice as we passed. I am sure it was the same girl. As I passed the parked car, she said hello again and we exchanged pleasantries. She struck me as one of the "loud" Maltese types.

As I passed into the bar, some boys were playing "grab-ass," which ceased abruptly as soon as they saw me. I plunked the case of empties down next to the bar. There was a pleasant young girl behind the bar, a little chubby perhaps, in a blue cotton dress. She fled into the living space back of the bar. Soon a slender older woman with lean handsome features and grey hair immerged and began talking to me in excellent English. She seemed proud of Malta, asked what I was doing here, where I lived. I explained how we had come to move into Hal-Tmiem, because the English psychiatrist had to go to a hospital for an eye operation and he and his wife wanted to have someone around to care for the cat. His name is Dr. Roberts. The woman expressed interest and sympathy, and obviously wanted to pump me for more information. As I extracted myself with a full case of beer, she hoped I would have a pleasant time and that my wife and I would return to the bar. The young bucks in the corner were silent all during this.

Returning to Hal-Tmiem, I passed the girl once more and exchanged some more pleasantries.

Comment: Something like "beware of the first people who talk to you in a strange place"; Margret Mead's witches. Here, it may be that the people who talk to you are proud of their English, but doesn't that make them "outsiders" of a type?

Wednesday, July 5th

Morning trip to Valletta with Marcia, to get meat for the week. I left the car at Mr. Fenech's for a wash and walked to meet her at the market. She was not there when I arrived, but soon came huffing up. On her way she had stopped at the bank to make some enquiries and no one had paid any attention to her. She said she had yelled "sheiit" in a loud voice and stomped out. When it became obvious that the amount of meat was becoming monstrous, I agreed to get the car and return to the market, which I did, driving down King's Way and across Archbishop Street and around to the market on

Market Street. A little man helped her carry the meat to the car. She had spent 6 pounds on meat and she could hardly lift it. 6 pounds is about $16 American.

That evening Johnny came by with some sea urchin eggs, which he split for us. Supper was late and he sat with us while Marcia and Norma at the urchins. I tasted a spoonful, but I said it didn't taste like anything. Johnny cracked up. Then I told him how I had again mispronounced a Maltese word, making it come out "dirty."

Once Mary had told me to come along with her to get some bread and had told me what to say to the baker. Then, on Monday June 12, when we had Johnny and family o supper, and when we were passing the bread, I thought I recognized the word again. Then, the next day, Mary was washing the clothes in the bathtub next to my room. Somehow the subject of bread came up – she had asked if we needed any bread today- and I say "Yes, go and get "obla" instead of "obza." She said "No, you told me a dirty word" and returned abruptly to her washing. In a minute she came back with a little smile- I had asked her what it meant and she wouldn't tell me. She then said that "obla" meant "the woman, she is pregnant." Later, I told Marcia and Norman and we looked it up. The word stems from obb, the breast. Later, I told this story to Johnny and he did a double-take, bobbing his head down with pursed lips and breaking out into laughter. Evidently it was a very bad word, something like "knocked-up" in English. Later, when we were sitting around the table eating rabbit in the Bussketti during the Mnaria, he related the incident to Joe Fenech and his friends and the really seemed to get a big kick out of it.

The second time this mistake occurred was while Mary and I were talking around 1 PM, Saturday, July 1, while waiting for Joe Attard to appear. I had taken a list of words to Mary, Paula's sister (name: Abella? I think she told me "Fenech" when we were sitting on the wall at Mnaria- why?) and was pronouncing them for her. Then we came to a word I heard Johnny Maniscalco used which means "ghost" and also "look." The word was "hares," but I had written it down wrong in my notebook, and I said "hara" instead. Mary laughed and said "you told me a dirty word again." I looked it up later, and found that "hara" means dung, excrement; shit, in other words. I related this incident to Johnny at the supper table and he folded up. I think he enjoys us very much, as we do him.

Comment: There must be a lot of dirty words in Maltese, or else I have a dirty mind. Or else Mary had a dirty mind, because my pronunciation is not distinct and could be skewed towards a less objectionable word. I am incapable of making Freudian slips in Maltese as yet, yes?

Actually, I don't really think Mary has a dirty mind, but you must admit it makes a good theory. The pattern-seeking imagination sometimes overdoes it.

After supper, we packed up the tape recorder and stuff, and went once more to Lucy's bar, to see if a tape had been made of the serata of the evening before. Johnny agreed come with us and left his Lamberetta motorbike in the garage.

Follows the tale of Lucy's bar on the night of Wednesday, July 5th.

The "Lucky bar," usually referred to as "Aunt Lucy's Bar" after the roly-poly little woman who owns it, is one of the Maltese singing bars. It is located in Marsa, down the street next to the Freedom Press and off to the left at end of a dead end cobblestone road. It is a typical "cantina" type of bar, small and rectangular, with tables and benches along the sides and a bar at the far end. To the left of the bar is an entrance to the living quarters next door, which contains a kitchen, a stair way and a sitting room. It is usually very clean and freshly painted.

Lucy's Bar is inhabited by an extended family of prostitutes. Lucy is the madam, and she rules 4 or 5 female relations with an iron fist. The non-relatives include Chedda of the magnificent voice whose decibel level has spoiled every tape recording Marcia Herndon has attempted (Marcia has been trying to re-record her ever since we've been here, which explains our presence in the bar, besides our curiosity as to what had taken place during the serata of the evening before) and also a young, slender and rather attractive girl of about 20 with reddish hair.

Act 1, Scene 1

As we pull into the alley, two singers are discovered, Laus and Amar, plunking on a single guitar and singing improvised verses. Laus, who was playing the guitar, is an extremely handsome young man, slender, dark, with long black hair and large eyes a la Cornell Wilde. He was Marcia's informant two years ago and is somewhat out of the singing scene, although I understand his is an excellent singer. I think perhaps he is a little too intelligent for a singer. The other man is known as Amar. He is big, slightly stupid (according to Marcia, he is he Florence Foster Jenkens of the singers and is only tolerated because he makes so many mistakes). Amar has a protruding lower jaw, as if he didn't have any upper teeth. As we passed them, Laus laughed and switched to include some reference to "Marcia," which I clearly heard. We parked the car and walked back to them. Johnny proceeded to Lucy's. Laus and Amar had been singing out on the street in front of another bar. Marcia and Norma asked him to go with us to Lucy's, and he got up and walked around the corner as if he would come. Then he changed his mind, especially when he learned we were with Johnny. Johnny belongs to a different faction of signers, and although there is some antagonism, it is usually confined to singing and does not ordinarily prevent singers from fraternizing with each other. The plot thickened immediately. We left Laus and went into Lucy's.

Act 1, Scene 2:

Lucy's was deserted, except for Johnny and Lucy herself, who tended bar for us. Johnny immediately bought us a round of drinks. It is impossible to stop him from spending his money on us. We must be into him for about £20 by now. We talked to Lucy for a little while, through Johnny, because she doesn't (appear) to speak much English. Lucy said she would try to arrange for Chedda to meet Marcia the following Sunday, and that she had a tape already of Chedda's singing which she would loan to Marcia, if the arrangements didn't work out. The conversation then turned to me (recitative). Was I a doctor also? Yes? What did I do? Norma explained I was someone very good with the tape recorded, with the electricity, the radio. And with the TV? Yes, I said, also the TV. I knew damn well what was going to happen next. (Significant horn calls, here, over tremolo strings).

Well, you see we have this TV set and it's no good, because the screen, it is covered with rice? Rice? Yes, rice, little white things on the screen. You mean there are little white things on the TV screen? Yes, on the screen. We call it "snow" in America. Here it is called "rice." (trio, with Johnny interpreting and adding his own comments.)

Aria Bravuro: Ottavio (bass), singing "What could be causing the rice on the TV screen", Lucy: "You got drills, you got shavers, you got saws and lathes and neighbors, they make trouble, many trouble, I can do you no big favor."

Interjection (recitative) Yes, but the TV man came and it used to work and now it doesn't work and... (Johnny) come on, you want to see it? Let's go.

Exit Ottavio, Johnny stage right through curtained door. Lights up on split stage, bar to right, parlor, stairs and roof to left.

Act II, Scene I. Gran'scena doppio.

Johnny took me into the parlor where I discovered a stocky man slightly balding, starring at a TV set. Follows an animated conversation, with Johnny translating, and the man, Mose Chasa (Lucy's son and a guitarist with the singers), asking questions in excellent English. Carmen, his sister, short, plump with large eyes and shoulder length frizzy hair (looks very much like Lucy) turns the TV to the Italian station, which as it develops is the only station with the rice. There's an extended explanation about atmospheric disturbances. But the station was received very well, no rice, before the repair man came with a new aerial. Maybe it is the direction of the antenna? I'm being watched by an attractive prostitute who is sitting in the corner next to the door, holding a child in her lap. Anyway, she has a nice smile. Mose: "come on, you want to see it? Let's go." He gets up and starts out the room. Johnny follows, say's "come on." Looks like he knows his way around the house. We go up two flights of cracked marble stairs. On both landings, there are two blue doors to either side and some paintings (bad). I slip on the steps and almost fall, because they are uneven, and I feel foolish and clumsy.

Lucy, Norma and Marcia talk for a while (counter point), then go to sit down at a table. Lucy comes out and joins them. Did Lucy get the postcard they sent? The postcard from America? Yes, the postcard, etc. yes, she go the postcard. How nice. It made us very happy. Yes it is very hot tonight. You know, there isn't much business these days. Not so many customers. (I learned later from Laus, that Lucy is overcharging for beer and whisky. This is part of the reason he didn't want to go with us.)

Carmen leaves the parlor and joins trio in bar. Attractive prostitute takes child out the parlor door into the street and sits the child up on the trunk of a parked car.

Scene 2: The roof above, the bar below. Molto presto e parlando.

The roof is dark and the floor is divided with small rows of stone. Clotheslines are strung this way and that. Towering above the penthouse is a long pole with two antennas, which has two thick white wires leading over the side of the roof to the parlor below. The antenna is aligned like all the rest. The TV man said that one of the wires was shorting out from the rain. This could be so. Yes. Mose: "But once a TV man said it was the wire, and I got an RAF chap to look at the set and he found it was a small condenser. Yes, some repairmen are thieves; the same as car mechanics. Yes, well come over here, there is my house, and you see I have separate poles one for Rediffusion, one for the Italian. It is better, yes? O.K. we go now. Ara il wire" (punchline from a joke). We go back down stairs, Johnny slips on the same step I had stumbled over on the way up. "Ara step." I don't know if he felt foolish. Voices from the bar shrill, harsh, crescendo molto. We go out into the bar, and the cast is reassembled for the grand concert finale of the second act.

Enter two buffoons, dimly visible off stage. Voices: attractive prostitute hustling. Lucy and Carmen frown. She ought not to do that in the street. No, not in the street. (shouts) "Hey you, come in the bar". Carmen: Illustria Madonna, is that my regular? Norma: Where are Ottavino and Johnny, what is all the shouting about? (She doesn't know we are on the roof, looking at TV antennas and watching wires.) Marcia: I think, maybe, Ottavino and Johnny are in trouble, yes? Lucy:" Hobla, not in the street. Haven't I told you before"? (Enter attractive prostitute, now mad) "What do you mean"? Lucy and Carmen: (furioso) "We mean, don't hustle in the street". Marcia:" Where are Ottavino and Johnny"? Noma: "Should we rescue them"? Attractive prostitute: "What do you mean, don't hustle in the street- What do you think this is, an ice-cream parlor?" "Don't ----- with me you ------- or I'll ---- you back to where I ---- (affetuoso e con alcuna licenza) Norma: "Where's Johnny"? Marcia: "Where's Otto"?

Tableau:

Johnny, Norma, Otto on bench behind table next to the bar, Marcia is on chair facing in. Mose pauses at bar, Lucy, Carmen, Attractive prostitute standing, gesturing, and talking in loud deep (for women) voices. Mose finally walks over to Attractive prostitute, plucks a fold of her frilly white blouse above the bra strap (you can see her black bra underneath) and says in effect, "come on you, out." Grand exit through curtained door to parlor. Argument increases, continues. Two small children, a tiny boy and a chubby little girl with big black eyes and little golden rings in her pierced ears come out as if repelled by the scene within. They toddle about. The little girl comes to sit with us for a while.

Above the uproar in the back, Johnny tells us some of his remarkable stories. About how one night Lucy asked him to come behind the bar and help because it was so busy, and he found she had three "tail-of-the-bull" stashed under the counter- blackjacks! Lucy is too hard on everyone. Johnny tells the tale of the German bomb he ploughed over in his Father's field, and how the British bomb squad man sweated as he defused it, and told him "when you ploughed over that bomb, that day you were born." The tale of the Canadian pilot who, when he saw his life was finished (no fuel, no bullets) crashed his plane into the Italian fighter he was doing battle with. The Italian survived the crash, and when the soldiers came to get him he shot at them with his pistol. In the background, the argument subsides into mutters and grunts. Johnny tells how his grandfather who as partially deaf, and couldn't hear the air raid sirens, was shot by a plane as he was out in his field. He escaped by jumping behind a rubble wall, and then over again as the plane returned for another run at him from the opposite direction.

Scene 3:

We finish our drinks and depart. As we go out from the alley in our car, Laus and Amar are still singing. Everybody waves and says "Chau," "Goodnight." We drive offstage, a little to the left of center.

The above has been slightly enlarged from life, but not much. Everybody trips over the same wires. Ara il wire.

According to Marcia and Norma, the joke about "ara il wire" has two versions, one in which you say "watch the wire" after someone has already hit it, and one version in which you say "watch the wire" and someone looks up and trips into a hole.

Thursday, July 6th

In the morning, off to Mdina. Marcia and Norma drive me over. A busy morning ahead, cataloguing part books. Father Azzopardi said it made him nervous. It makes me dizzy, especially when he starts buzzing when I'm trying to spell something. Hope he will take me to see the bells soon, perhaps on Monday when I return. (Haven't decided what to do with this material yet, certainly a notice about the collection.) Lots of work to do back home, locating the composers. I am disappointed because it seems more and more likely that the Mss we had catalogued are only copies of the printed parts to preserve them. Father Azzopardi said that formerly, 60-70 years ago, there was no radio and the people looked to the church to supply music. Even theatricals were done in the church. This perhaps in spite of Pius X Moto against instruments other than the organ in church? But, with the Rediffusion, interest in music in the church has declined and it is difficult to arrange for performances. He is really convinced that someone ought to do something on Francesco Azzopardi (1748-1809), a Maltese composer also famous in Europe in his time.

Norma and Marcia met me at the entrance to Mdina, a little late. Going down the road, Marcia speeded up, passed a car at 45 and started wiggling the steering wheel back and forth. I blew up and told her to behave. Norma said something about that's how you drive and I said nothing. Maybe I do go a little fast, but I do understand English and if someone says "slow down, you're making me nervous," I will. Foo!

In the afternoon, I'm off to Tony's bar in Marsaxloxx to meet Joe Attard. I meet Mary and Lena coming down the road. I had gone up and taken picture of St. Peter's church and had my camera. I threatened them with it and they half turned around in protest. Lena was wearing curlers. I meet Joe and drove him home again. He seemed much less shy. We talked for a while about the pattern of the clock bells which he had laboriously written out and which I had already figured out from the information he had given me before. I copied it down anyway, to please him. I then began to ask him questions from the outline I had prepared, but he could not help much, because, he said, the Sexton didn't tell him these things. I asked if we could both get together with the Sexton and save Joe some trouble. Joe agreed, but said the first time he had tried to get the sexton to go with him to my house but he was too shy. We talked a while about the school project he had done on the history of Marsaxloxx. Then Joe said we could go now and see if the Sexton was sitting in front of his house. If he wasn't there, we could go tonight at 9:10 to find him (why such a curious time?). When we returned to Marsaxlokk, Joe directed me down he ally just above the church, in search of the Sexton.

But the Sexton wasn't there, so I dropped Joe in front of his house with the blue door at 16 Zejtun Road. We agreed to meet that evening.

Complications set in over the use of the car. Marcia wanted to go back and talk to Laus, so we agreed that Marcia and Norma should drop me in Marsaxloxx and pick me back up around 10:30 or 11. I was deposited a little early, about 9:45. I walked for a bit, lit a pipe and settled myself on the stone bench on the Quay across from Tony's Aviator bar. Joe did not show up. I walked up the street a ways to see if he was coming. Finally I went in Tony's, bought a paper and digested it complete. Still no Joe. I went back to the Quay and sat until 10:15 when Joe finally came ambling up. Tony had just closed up. Joe said his mother had awakened him and told him the American was waiting. He said he got up to meet me, but fell asleep. He asked why I hadn't left, and I explained someone else had the car and I was stuck there until they returned. He was very apologetic.

Was he trying to "shake" me, i.e. discourage me by standing me up, and later decided he would have to meet me after all? I don't think this was his motive. He had said earlier that he "had some trouble at work today" and repeated this for an excuse. We were soon joined by a friend, a boy of about Joe's age, lighter complexion and long sandy hair. He spoke better English than Joe, and was quite talkative and friendly. He and Joe sat with me on the stone bench until 11:45, when I gave Marcia and Norma up for lost or dunk or something and started walking home. I had the feeling they would have sat with me all night to keep me company. It was a little cold and damp, and I was getting anxious about them as well as Marcia and Norma and so I left and went off walking down the road. It was getting dark. I heard the evening Angelus as I passed up the hill. An extra, louder peal ended the ringing, the Maltese "punctuation" stroke, ("that's all!)

Some of the things I learned from Joe and his friend:

1. Boissevian, the standing authority on Malta, (Hal-Farrug, p. 56) is mixed up about the bells. I showed this passage to Joe at home and he said some of it made no sense, i.e. "The Angelus bell then rings a call to prayer at 8 in the morning, again at noon and at sunset, when the Ave Maria is rung to

mark the end of the day". First of all, according to Joe, the Angelus is a prayer, not a bell, and therefore the Angelus bell cannot ring the Ave Maria (also a call to prayer). Earlier, Boissevian says the bells ring to announce to those outside the important stages of the mass. Joe says this is true only on festal days, not every day.

2. I had noticed as I waited for Joe that only the first half of the clock patterns were striking, i.e. the divisions of the hour, but not the hour. For example, 10+15 was only one bell, and not one bell followed by 4 bells (which indicates the hour). I told Joe and his friend this, but they would not believe me until the clock struck again. I had thought there was some switch the Sexton could turn that would eliminate the hour in the evening and night. They thought, on the contrary, that the clock was broken, and they were going to tell the Sexton.

Friday, July 7

Today, I learned that there are 52 parishes in Malta, 17 in Gozo. The number of churches is unknown, for there are sometimes many churches in a parish, for example Valletta has about 20. The person I spoke to, suggested I contact Mon. Prof. Colliero at the University and speak to the procurator of the Cathedral Museums at St. John's and Mdina. I asked about the Archbishop's office, and was given directions. He has his headquarters on Archbishop's Street (where else?).

Later in the afternoon, I returned to Valletta (about 4 pm) and went to the Archbishop's, but the caretaker said all was closed for the day and I could return at 9 in the morning. The same is true for the museum and St. John's. Moral: if you don't get it done before 12:30, forget it.

I noticed groups of British military on leave in the city. About 900 British Commandos have returned to Malta. Several shops on Kingsway were displaying military tidbits. The soldiers struck me as very young, 18-20, boys, really. They were obvious by their clothing: woolen pants, long-sleeved shirts, pull-over sweaters- and especially, by the way they walked, throwing out the elbows and arms, swaying from side to side and bumbling all over the street. One quickly learns not to stick elbows out and swagger in Valletta, one of the most crowded cities I have ever been in. I don't believe I have ever been hit by any Maltese on the street, although I have, on several occasions, swatted one or two with a package or a protruding arm.

At St. John's, I did learn that the procurator's name was Mon. Bonnini.

Back up: Joe's friend knew about the bell maker, Guliano, although he did not know the name. He said Guliano closed his shop whenever he cast a bell and would not let anyone see how he did it, and that when he died, he took his secrets with him. He suggested I look in the Royal Library for information. Also, he said earlier, that if I wanted to see any bell whatever, I should get in touch with the parish priest and he would arrange it gladly. So easy. Joe's friend knew about the Neolithic remains and the museums. He also repeated a story I had heard from Mary G., about the bones of large animals in a certain museum, and how Malta was once part of Africa.

Also while I was waiting for Joe, I think I heard the Tal-Imwiet rung at 10 PM in a medium low- pitch bell (Carmena?) it was 1234, 1234, 1234, 12. I believe this was also rung at 9 PM: however, I think there were only 12 strokes, and the bell was higher in pitch (Stella Maris?). The bell at 9 may have been Ave Maria.

Saturday, July 8

Hot after interview with France Gatt, Sexton at Marsaxlokk parish church. Joe Attard interpreted.

1. Dates of bells: he doesn't know exactly. Victoria bell here from St. Dominic's in Valletta, purchased more than twenty years ago. Stella Maris purched about 30 years ago from St. Julian's in Sliema.
2. The failure of the clock to struck the hour last Thursday night (July 6). I couldn't catch what Joe said too well, something like "well he makes them." I asked if he stopped them, Joe sad "he makes them go." I gather the Sexton fixed them.
3. Tal-Imwiet: rung on P-Antika except day before feast and feast day, when rung on Victoria. Twelve strokes are used. On January 1st, Tal-Imwiet is rung at 8:15 PM. Every 15 days a quarter hour is subtracted from the time. By May 8th, the time is 10 PM. The bells are rung at 10 PM until August 15th, when a quarter hour is added every 15 days, until 8 PM is reached by November 21st. Then, the time is reversed, subtracting 15 minutes every 15 days. Damn! Then is it reversed again to reach 8:15 by January 1st? Didn't see this one coming.
4. The Ave Maria is rung whenever the sun goes down. Time varies according to season, 5-7 o'clock. P-antika is rung with 12 strokes.
5. Friday at 3 PM the bells are rung for the death of Jesus, for 5 minutes. I couldn't make myself clear to Joe on this point, but the pattern I heard at 3 PM on Friday, June 23rd went something like:

(ex.5)

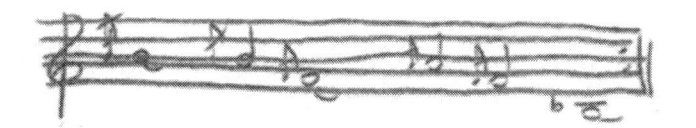

Mr. Gatt, the Sexton, said a mota was rung in this order: 1. Marija, 2. Carmina, 3. P-antika (Ruzarja), 4. Stella Maria, 5. Victoria. Now, the problem is this: Marija has no rope. It is attached to the clock and must be rung by hand. To ring a mota in this order there would have to be one person on each bell, because no one can run fast enough from bell-tower to bell tower to execute either a mota or the pattern I heard. What I heard might be an abbreviated version, rung from below. It does not seem likely that 5 people would gather on the roof to ring the mota every Friday, or does it? Maybe so. It may depend sometimes on the number of boys the Sexton is able to round up. I still do not think I have a complete explanation, because a mota is a bell pattern that begins with one bell, slowly, then accelerated after about 25 strokes, when the second bell begin slowly and then speeds up and so forth. What the dickens did I hear, then? I am quite positive I heard it; L-orazjumr? This is a new ringing Joe did not mention before. The dictionary spells it Ordinarju, perhaps, calendar of divine offices? Tgarbina- communion. Orazzjoni? I can't find this spelling in the dictionary. Why is it my perceptual information- i.e. what I hear, what I see in the dictionary – is sometimes in conflict with what they tell me? A common problem, I'd say.

This ringing is also described as a mota. It lasts for 15 minutes, from 8:45 to 9 PM on Thursday, to celebrate the memory of the communion of Christ at the last supper. The order is: 1, Victoria, 2, Stella Maris, 3, P-antika, 4, Carmina. Again, this would perhaps require 4 people upstairs on the bells. From a remark of Joe's I gather the sexton sometimes pulls two, maybe three bells himself, from downstairs. Joe himself rings the bells from time to time, and he said he sometimes rings two. I gather the bells are hard to ring from downstairs and it takes great skill and probably no little strength to move the heavy clappers via thick ropes. It must take good timing, too, because of the time delay.

I told Mr. Gatt through Joe I thought he was a very good bell ringer. Joe agreed, and said he was the best ringer in all Malta, because he knew to ring the bells, if too hard, would not sound good.

Mr. Gatt said the largest bell in Malta is at Brikirkara. Zejtun's bell is second to that of Birkirkara.

The Sexton from Zejtun comes over to ring the bells during the village festal. He is paid 6 pounds from 3 AM to 10 PM. This was in response to a question I asked, if he knew other sextons. I must ask if he himself goes and rings the bells for festal elsewhere. My guess is Zejtun. This must be complex, for very parish church has different bells, larger, smaller, fewer or more. Or, Is the number and character of bells standardized?

Mr. Gatt said he learned to ring the bells from the former Sexton when he was a small boy. He said (or this is what I got) he did not know if the bells in B'Buga, the new ones, were made of bronze. The best clappers- "tongues"- were made of iron.

Context: I decided not to go priesting today, but rather to catch up on the two - week gap in my notes. I worked all day. It was a little unsettling to relive, as it were, the events of those weeks. I finished about 7 PM, rested for a while. Marcia & Norma went after Johnny M. because they wanted to ask him some questions to clear up some things in their notes. We had supper together, and then I left to meet Joe Attard at Tony's bar as arranged. Tony said he went about 8:30 to meet me because he was so late the last time. As I drove up and parked on the quay, I saw him walking down the street to Tony's from his house. He was talking to a rather pitiful man, dirty and ill clothed; sitting on the curb in front of Tony's with a small cart from which he sold peanuts. I had noticed him Thursday evening during the long wait for Joe. Joe came over and gestured and said: "This is my father." I said hello. I was embarrassed, and I think Joe was too. We walked over to the church where we met the Sexton, Mr. Gatt, a large man in his fifties perhaps, short greying hair, very jolly person, with huge patches of black hair growing out of his ears. He wore a black band on his left sleeve. I had met him several times before, and it seemed to me the band was always around his arm. Does it matter?

Joe said the Sexton should come to my house, as the square was not the proper place to talk about these matters, and he didn't want to be seen. However, I would have to get him back to the church in time to ring the Tal-Imwiet at 10:00. We walked back to the car. Joe and the Sexton conversed in Maltese. Joe does not mumble when speaking Maltese. The Sexton barely fit into the front seat of the Triumph 1100. He seemed very amused and laughed freely. Back at Hal-Tmiem, Marcia, Norma, and Johnny M. were sitting on the veranda. I introduced Mr. Gatt to Marcia and Norma and he said "I don't speak English." Johnny M. came up and jokingly introduced himself. He knew the Sexton, of course. I took Joe and Mr. Gatt inside and opened three Hopleaf beers and we settle down to some questions. Joe and he spent a lot of time talking. Sometimes I felt Joe was having a little trouble making him understand. On the way over, Joe said "He is a good man, he will help everybody."

About 9:30 Joe nudged me and said I should get another drink for Mr. Gatt, because he liked Hopleaf. I complied. This is the fastest I ever saw a Maltese guest drink beer. When we stood up to go, Joe told me jokingly, "you make him drunk." After some goodbyes to Marcia and Normal and Johnny M. (who, according to Norma as kidding him, saying I hope you like my place and will return, or something like that), we got back into the Triumph and drove back. Joe reached over and wound down the window for the Sexton as we pulled away. The Mr. Gatt said it was a good time for driving, in the evening, that he enjoyed it very much. It may be a wrong impression, but I had the feeling he did not ride in cars very much.

As we pulled into Marsaxloxx, I drove in past his house, in order to deposit him right back in front of the door where he would have to ring the bells. Some people were sitting on the doorsteps, and I had the impression he was embarrassed to be seen riding in a car, because he put his hand up to his forehead and laughed. Probably the craziest thing he has ever done. After we had let him out and said goodbye, Joe asked to be driven to the beach. On our way, we saw the Grech sisters (naturally) and I honked.

Earlier, at the house, we made arrangements to meet at the same time next Saturday, the 15th.

Afterthoughts: I should not have asked the Sexton how he learned to ring the bells; personal direct question. I should have said, "Suppose I want to learn to ring the bells, what do I do?" I should have found out who the former sexton was- I.e. was it his father or a relative? It is a family trade?

Sunday, June 9th

Drive to Mdina for walking and pictures, and then drive straight to Hamrun (more modern city, wide streets) around to Pieta and Sliema and home; lunch and sun.

Summary of information about the Marsaxloxx Parish Church Bells.

- I. The Bells: There are 5 bells. Two bells hang in the left tower (as you face the church) and three are placed in the right tower

    A. Right tower bells

        i. <u>Victoria</u>- the largest ("Il-Kbira")

Maker: Guilano
Date: (?)
Hung: (?) c. 1950 "20 years ago"- "25 years ago" – Father Delicata
Comment: Almost too large for tower, hits edges when rung
Function: On prima or festal days, Victoria substituted for other bells.
Origin: Purchased from St. Dominic's in Valletta, when new bells were installed there.

ii. Ruzarja- the old one ("P-antika")
Maker: Fonderia + St. Carlo (Italy)
Hung: The only bell of the church for a long time.
Date: (?)
Comment: Hangs in front of tower, out over edge.
Function: used for Tal-Imwiet, Ave Maria (8 AM), Sunday masses, 25 strokes every 15 minutes. Ave Maria (Sunset)

B. Left tower bells

i. Carmena – the medium ("fostanna")
Maker: Guliano
Date: (?)
Hung: (?) c. 1950
Origin: purchased from St. Dominic's
Comment: Hangs on left edge of right-hand tower.
Function: (a) attached to clock mechanism. Rings hour, (b) rung from left –hand tower foyer by rope which runs across roof. Used for Pater Noster at 6:15 AM. Used 4 PM for catechism.

ii. <u>Stella Maris- (no Maltese name)</u>
Maker: Guliano
Date: 1834 (inscription on bell)
Origin: Purchased from St. Julian's in Sliema (sexton)
Comments: large bell, about the size of Ruzarja, if not larger. Hangs like Ruzarja on front edge of tower. Hand rung via rope from foyer.
Function: Seems to be used only in the multiple bell motas. Never rung by itself?

iii. <u>Marija- ("Al-mejtin") – for the dead.</u>
Maker: Guliano
Date: 1885 (inscription)
Origin: Purchased from St. Dominic's
Comments: Hung on left window of tower. A rather small bell, (estimated diameter- 2 feet) it has the highest pitch. There is about a foot long chip missing from the outside rim. A small boy was said to have rung it too hard.
Function: (a) connected to clock, strives the quarter hour. (b) Marija is not connected to the foyer by rope. Its main function is to sound the Trapasjoni, the bell for the dead. It is used in a mota only on 3 PM Friday, when a Mota is rung for the death of Christ. Marsha wondered if it were the "dead" bell because it was cracked, but it turned out not to be the case.

II. Clock Bells. The two smallest bells, Marija and Carmena are connected to the clock in the right-hand tower and are rung by hammers. The clock itself is run by 4 weights suspended on ropes. The force of gravity provides the energy. The weights must be wound up by pulleys every 2 days.

There are 2 divisions to the clock bells. The first strokes, rung on Maria, the smallest bell, ring the quarter hour:

4 strokes = on the hour
1 stroke = 1st quarter (15 minutes past the hour)
2 strokes = 2nd quarter (30 minutes past the hour)
3 strokes = 3rd quarter (45 minutes past the hour)

The second division, rung on Carmena, indicates the hour according to a 6 hour code, i.e., Carmena never rings more than 6 times, and begins again with one stroke at 7 AM and 7 PM.
The cycle is:

1 o'clock & 7 o'clock = 1 stroke
2 o'clock & 8 o'clock = 2 strokes
3 o'clock & 9 o'clock = 3 strokes
4 o'clock & 10 o'clock = 4 strokes
5 o'clock & 11 o'clock = 5 strokes
6 o'clock & 12 o'clock = 6 strokes

In this manner, 12:30, for example, would be two strokes on Marija and 4 strokes on Carmena.
All clocks in Malta do not use this system. The clock bells in Zejtun, rung by a convent church have a melody. Father Azzopardi in Mdina said the clocks there used a different pattern.

III. Bells of the calendar day:

    A. The Pater Noster: Formerly rung at 3:45 AM (3:30 on Sunday) but stopped by the order of the Archbishop and

moved to 6 AM (6:15), because (according to Joe Attard), tourism is a business and the tourists were complaining. The parish priest decides on the time because of the changing time of sunrise. Marsaxloxx is a fishing village, very much tied to the rise and setting of the sun.
Rung on Carmena, 25 strokes.
Both Johnny and Lena G. said there is still a single bell at 4 AM, to wake the fishermen.

B. Ave Maria: (Angelus) 8 AM, 12 strokes with P-antika (Ruzarja). "To pray the holy of rosaries." On prima or festal days, rung on Victoria.

C. Angelus – "Prayer of Angelus" 12 strokes with Victoria. On Saturday 24th, I noticed a two bell mota here. Maybe for weekend, or for dedication to the Sacred Heart of Jesus on the next day.

D. Catechism bell: 4 PM, ½ hour before Museum teaches children. (except Sunday when Catechism taught in church)

E. (?) 6:15 PM, c. 25 strokes for mass, at 6:30 rung on P-antika (Ruzarja)

F. Ave Maria: rung when sun goes down (sunset). 12 strokes on P-antika (Ruzarja), Victoria substituted on festal days. Time varies from 5 PM to 7 PM, according to season.

G. Tal-Imwiet: for the souls in purgatory. 12 strokes on P-antika. Changed to Victoria on festal days. i.e. day before festal day and festal day. The time at which Tal-Imwiet is rung changes. January 1st = 8:15. Every 15 days, 15 minutes is subtracted. By May 8th, he time is 10 PM. The time is held at 10 PM until August 15th, then, a quarter hour is added every 15 days, until 8 PM is reached by November 21st. Then, another quarter hour is subtracted, etc. I have not fully worked this out yet.

IV. Sunday Bells:
4 PM Mota rung on Ruzarja and Carmena by sexton. 15 minutes. Sexton then joins others in church for rosary prayers. Rosary takes 15 minutes. The Sexton then rings for catechism in church at 4:15. The catechism begins at 4:45.

5:45. 15 minutes to mass at 6:25 strokes with Ruzarja
6:45. 15 minutes to mass at 7:
8:00. 15 minutes to mass at 8:15

Question: Is Ruzarja rung every 15 minutes from 5:45 to when? (During the Sunday evening masses) This from Joe Attard.

V. Trapasjoni: the bell for the dead. 25 strokes with Marija.
Time: 11:45 AM: someone not from Marsaxloxx
12:00 PM: someone from Marsaxloxx (before time strokes)
5:30 PM: signals?
In old days, bell was to summon hearse to church.
Also rung after funeral, to accompany body to grave. In Marsaxloxx, bells stop when hearse (or horse drawn still) passes St. Peter. (no cemetery in Marsaxloxx.)

VI. L-Orazjomr: Mota for 15 minutes every Thursday, to remember communion of Christ at Last Supper.
Order: Victoria, Stella Maris, Ruzjara, Carmena.
Time: 8:45 to 9 PM, (Thursdays)

VII. (?) Fridays at 3 PM. Mota for death of Christ.
Order: Marija, Carmena, Ruzjara, Stella Maris, Victoria.
This may be the highest to the lowest pitches. Noticed a slower pattern on Friday June 23.

Monday, July 10

I overslept by a half-hour at least this morning; kept awake by the bugs and the vision of an enormous cockroach, which I tried to swat off the bedroom wall and missed. He disappeared under the other bed, not to be seen again. Guess I scared him. The traffic noise is considerable as well. The road outside Hal-Tmiem is very narrow- so narrow you could spit across it on a windy day. I am constantly awakened by the passage of cars and huge trucks careening by, blowing their horn for the intersection ahead and tearing rubber off their tires as they hit the brakes. The Maltese driver is someone to be reckoned with. Often I have been startled by a car approaching in my lane, and only a quick mental calculation convinces me I am driving in the right lane after all. The temptation to swing over to the right hand side of the road is strong in an emergency. When you drive down the narrow sidewalk-less streets at night, the headlights pick up rows of bare feet protruding into the streets. The do not retract for your passage, these Maltese feet. Run over them at your own risk, they seem to say. The Maltese sit on their doorsteps in the evenings, and since the doorsteps are one step down to the street, there is no room for both feet and cars. I don't know how people get around on this tight little island. In fact, most of them just stay where they are and leave the driving to us! In Birzebbuga, the people try to throw themselves under your wheels, particularly in the vicinity of the Sea Breeze Restaurant. No matter which way you have turned, someone has just stepped nonchalantly in front of you (or in back of you while parking). I have hypothesized that if in the evening, you don't find many people in Marsaxloxx, they have probably gone to throw themselves beneath the wheels of cars in Birzebbuga. The main square in Zejtun is an alternative, I think. Even the Maltese dread driving in this square.

However, I took myself off to the University this morning and found it with no difficulty at all.

The trick seems to be to drive fast enough so that you will get ahead of the traffic and have time to stop to make a decision at an intersection. I had been directed to Mons. Prof. Colliero by the man in the office of statistics. I finally located his office by asking one student and two secretaries. The Mos. Prof. was busy in his office with an examination. After a few minutes, the secretary suggested that I come back in a half hour, having refreshed myself in the canteen. I took myself off to the library instead and looked up some articles on bells in the Ency. Am. and Groves. When I returned to Mons. Prof. Colliero's office at about 11:30, both the secretary and the Mons. Prof. had left, although I did have a sprightly conversation with a maid cleaning there, as to when they might return. Very clever and most astute. I shall call this ploy the Maltese shunt. It will not work, for I will appear even earlier tomorrow, and they will be most contrite.

Then, I drove on into Valletta to visit the Archbishop office for a while. It is very necessary to have alternative plans of action in mind, I can tell. The street down to the Archbishopric on Archbishop Street (where else) was blocked by some falling masonry- they were tearing something down and would not let me pass. So I had to back track and short cut through Strait Street where all the bars of prostitution are. It made a strange contrast. After some minutes and pas de deux with the door tender and one other official, I was taken to Mons. Bonnicini, who assured me there were no central records of bells, nor any written standards and rules for bell ringing. Except, he added, that the Archbishop had prohibited the ringing of the Pater

Noster before 6 AM. It was formerly at 4 AM. At first he tried to say that the edict or whatever was not written down, then said it was and that it could possibly be found. (i.e. not today, please, he was busy- he really was.) We laughed at the thought of me having to climb out over tower railings, copying down dates and inscriptions. He said I would have to do my study parish by parish. He had shaken my hand when I introduced myself, and now he offered his hand again.

As I left, I thanked the doorkeeper again. I took a deviant path back to Kingsway Street, down almost to the quay, over a few streets and then up. The decorations for the feast of Valletta were being prepared. As I passed down on street I heard the busy tac-tac of hammers being lustily applied to some task ahead of me, and I thought that this was the most industrious sound I had heard to date in Malta ("take it easy, pal Inglesi" -a Maltese joke). As I neared the shop I saw some wooden planks stacked in one corner, and thought it must be a carpenter's shop. When I got in front, I saw two men pounding a coffin together, and inserting thin sheets of metal inside. Death is a very important business in a Catholic country.

Passing up to Kingsway again, I saw a crowd of people. Two girls passing me were talking about it in Maltese and I caught the word "Inglesa." When I reached the top of the street, a man with an ascot and a policeman were leading an attractive but limp young lady away. Don't know what happened.

Mons. Bonnici had given me the tile of a book I might consult in the Royal Library: Ferres, Achille: Descrizione storia della chiese di Malta e Gozo. Malta, 1866. I found the book (rather, someone scurried back in the stacks and found it for me), but I found I could not take it out as it was a reserve book. I took it into the reading area and perused it for a while and took some notes (notebook no. 2). It was a descriptive account of the churches in Italian. I found little about bells, only their number and some dedications. I returned the book at the desk. I had had to sign it out and the attendant checked it off as I left. As it was 12 noon by then, and since I was more than hungry, I treated myself to a pizza before returning to the car.

I decided to see if Johnny M. was in Marsaxloxx, because I wanted to find out when they were taking the boat out of the shop. Sure enough, I found him in his paint cap inside the brand-new boat on inside the St. Pius V Street open shop. He said he didn't know to tell me when the boat would be taken out and down to the water yet, and I said we Inglese would be coming out for bread every day any way and that we would check by. He seemed pleased to see me and said several times "you can come any time," which I guess is an invitation.

In the afternoon, Norma and Marcia dropped me off at Zejtun. I turned in the sewerage stamp to the police and made my way back to the church. I met a priest and asked directions to the parish priest's house, which I found in back of the church. It was No. 10 and decorated with a coat of arms bearing three fish and a wide brimmed hat overhead. These emblems appear over all parish and official residences, as I recognized this one as the same I had seen over the priest's house in Marsaxloxx and the Archbishopric.

No one answered the bell, for it didn't ring. Some times were announced in Maltese on a plaque, and I assumed the Archbishop wasn't in to the public until 4:30. I took myself around the building – i.e. the church, and examined the bell towers from below. Zejtun church is very large and impressive. The roof is not flat, but kind of egg-carton like with bulges:

(ex.6)

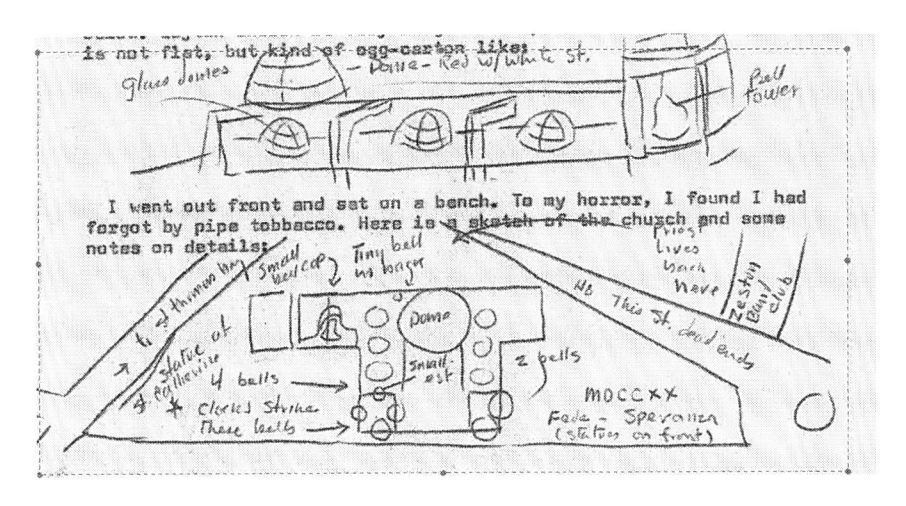

[Hand-drawn sketch with handwritten notes showing a church layout with bells, dome, and annotations including "glass domes", "is not flat, but kind of egg-carton like", "Dome - Red w/white st.", "Bell tower", "I went out front and sat on a bench. To my horror, I found I had forgot by pipe tobbacco. Here is a sketch of the church and some notes on details:", "Small bell cot", "Tiny bell in bag?", "4 bells", "statue of reliever", "Clock strike — These bells →", "Dome", "small alt", "2 bells", "MDCCXX", "Fede — Speranza (statues on front)", "Priest lives back", "Nave", "This St. dead end", "Vesting Boys Club"]

    I went closer to the church and found I could not photograph the front of the left transept building, which contained a bell cot and some single bell. As I came away, a pudgy old man in sunglasses and white shirt kept waving at me. I finally went over and asked what he wanted. He wanted to know why I was so interested in the church. I told him, because of the bells and excused myself. Witches, witches; polite Maltese would not ask questions.

    Back up: On my way around the church I entered cautiously thru the right transept and walked along the edge to the door. Several old men were sitting regarding the altar, one to each side, and maybe the altar is never left unattended at certain times? I paused at the back and blessed myself with holy water. I read the usual prohibition about women not wearing sleeveless blouses and short skirts in the church. I think the church is antagonistic to women. It seems to me that most of the skeletons incased in the altars were women, too (!).

    None of the bars or shops were open, except for the one on the corner were the young bucks gather to stick their feet into the narrow road to harass the traffic. I decided to walk around a bit, and I took off towards the place where the market is held, on the way out to the superhighway, to Valletta. Walking down the street I noticed a fine bell cot some building in the distance and decided to find it. I seemed to be off to the left somewhere. I got so interested in the old church in the market square, which had two old bells, one in the front and on in the back, that I got turned around and never found the place where the first set of bells was attached. However, the walk was pleasant, and I finally came out in the square again. I took a new aim on the bells and located them on what I think is a nunnery right on the street to the market. I backed up and took a picture, and also a picture of the old church.

I was seen by many people- bet I am the talk of the town. I returned to the square, and as it was 4:30, I made my way to the priest's house behind the church. The bell worked this time and I was admitted by a maid. Yes, the father was in. The house, maid, curtains and all, were almost identical to Father Delicata's office in Marsaxloxx. I introduced myself to the parish priest and explained my mission. I never learned his name. He is a small, balding man with large black eyes. He was sweating profusely and carried a stick fan like this:

(ex.7)

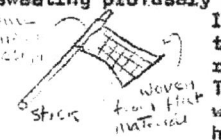

```
black eyes. He was sweating profusely and carried a stick fan
kxxkx Like this:                          I had seen several other
clergy carry this                         type of fan in a Zabbar and
Valletta. Which                           reminds me, earlier that
day on my way to                   woven  The Archbishopric, I had
seen two young men         stick  f...t   with grey shirts and white
collars holding                   material hands.
```

I had seen several other carry this type of fan in Zabbar and Valletta. Which reminds me, earlier that day on my way to the Archbishopric, I had seen two young men with grey shirts, white collars and black pants holding hands (!), walking down the street. Later found out they were Church novices, and that holding hands like that had nothing to do with their gender (or my business, for that matter).

The parish priest was very cooperative, and took me out the door. He was going to let me see the bells and copy the inscriptions. He moved very fast, like Father Azzopardi in Mdina. However, the maid called him back for a telephone call. The maid hissed at him. I think this is the common way of getting someone's attention. I had noticed this while I was in Panama. I remember a story one of my close friends had told me about meeting a girl in Japan. She waved at him and he thought she meant for him to go away, but he started out and she came and grabbed him by the arm. Another custom is a swishing sound used to call cats and dogs: "schi-wi-wi-wi-wi."

Anyway, when the priest returned from his phone call, he took me in the back door of the church, carefully locking it behind him. As we entered the nave, he told me to wait while he found a man, but when he returned, he said he could not find him. I asked if it was the Sexton, but I think he said it was the man who rang the bells, i.e. the Sexton does not always ring the bells? (Too much work in a large church?) What are the duties of a sexton, anyway- I must remember to ask Father next Saturday. Anyway, I was to return at 6:30 tomorrow and meet with the man in the nave.

After I thanked the priest, I went out the front door and went to have a beer in the Zejtun Band Club, which was open by now. I was left pretty much alone, except for one man in a hat who passed by and remarked, "Alright, governor, sketching?" I was drawing in my note book. Norma remarked after reading my notes, that I should have grabbed the guy, shown him my notes and grilled him about the bells! After I finished my beer, I walked home, pausing to take a picture of the convent that had the clock chimes.

The interior of the Band Club was like this:

(ex.8)

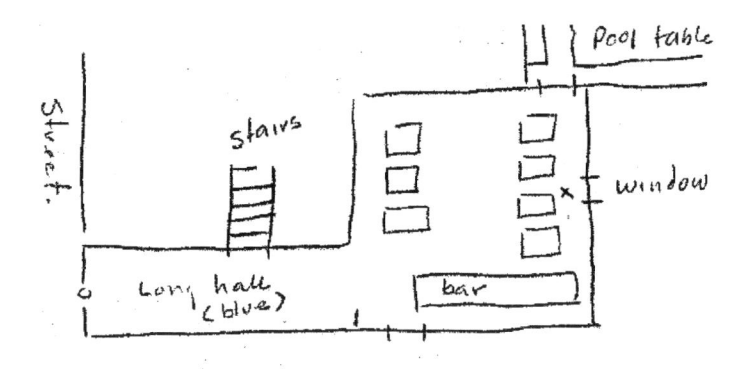

[Floor plan sketch: Street on left; stairs, long hall (blue), bar, window, pool table labeled within the layout.]

That evening, I went in to Marsaxloxx on an impulse to check on the Tel-Imwiet. At 10 PM the clock bells struck only he quarter hour, on Marija, which I thought sounded bad because of the crack. (Suppose I wanted to get a new bell. What would I do with Marija then?)

The Tal-Imwiet began shortly after the clock stroke, about 45 seconds or a minute. It was rung irregularly, I thought, the strokes being neither equally spaced nor grouped. The bell rang 13 times, instead of 12. The last stroke was a quick one, almost like a double stroke, which I thought was impossible from the foyer.

Several questions? Is the sexton careless? Any reason for 13 strokes instead of 12, on Jul 10? Was it the sexton ringing the bells or someone else? Joe said he sometimes rings the bells. It was only afterwards that I learned that the extra, final ring was meant as a punctuation, an "OK, we're done". This also happens after a sally of fireworks, meaning that everything was OK, no problems, etc.

Walking down the quay, I met Carminu B. and Johnny M. He asked if I knew who Carminu was, and I spewed out his full name. I think they were pleased. I walked them back to Pius V Street and then drove back to Hal Tmiem.

Some questions:

1. Do people in Marsaxloxx know what the names of the bells are?
2. The dates and figures of the ringing times of the Tal-Imwiet do not come out any way, according to what the Sexton said. Something is missing. How does Easter mess it up?
3. What about this fictitious wooden rattle that replaces bells on Good Friday and Easter Sunday, according to Boissevian? Has anyone heard of it?
4. Social status of the Sextant, in a supposedly equalitarian society? Does his duties at the church make him different, or "outside" the society. What else does he do?

Sexton: (Sacristan) A church officer having the care of the fabric of a church and is contents, and the duties of ringing the bells and digging graves. (In pop. use from the 16th century usu. = bell ringer and grave digger. (Ox Eng. Dict. Vol II 1944.)

What is the social status of a Sexton, particularly in a MLP town like Marsaxloxx? His affiliation with the church must affect people's behavior towards him. Is he married, with kids?

Tuesday, July 11^t

Just returned from a hectic day in Marsaxlokxx and Zejtun. It is 8:15 at night, and I am very tired, but I want to get this information down first.

First of all, the meeting with the bell ringer at Zejtun: I drove from Marsaxloxx back to Hal Tmiem, changed clothes, gobbled some cookies and arrived at the Zejtun church at about 6:25. I went in the left front door, walking quietly. Many people, well, some at least, had gathered and were staring fixedly at the altar. I crossed the left transept after blessing myself with the water. In the vestry I met the parish priest, who came up with a small man of about 45 or 50 with grey hair. There was some confusion about the huge keys. I learned later on (only after introducing myself) that his name was Grech. (Perhaps an exchange of names is too personal?) Mr. Grech is a very energetic fallow; agile as it turned out, and very knowledgeable about the bells. He genuflected at the altar and led me a merry chase up the isle to a tall metal door off the left tower. We went up a circular staircase over 90 steps, he said- I lost count after 51 because I had to concentrate to breathe (!). The steps were limestone and some of them were very worn. Finally, we came out on the roof, which is bumped like that of Marsaxloxx, but much larger. We went up into the left tower first.

The left tower contains four bells in a square:

(ex. 9)

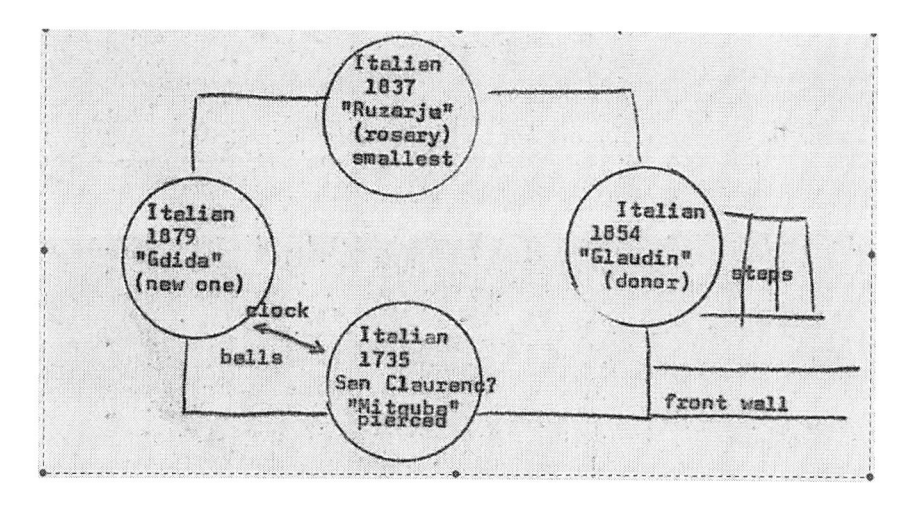

```
                    ┌──────────────┐
                    │   Italian    │
                    │    1837      │
         ┌──────────│  "Ruzarja"   │──────────┐
         │          │   (rosary)   │          │
         │          │   smallest   │          │
         │          └──────────────┘          │
   ┌─────────┐                          ┌─────────┐
   │ Italian │                          │ Italian │   ┌──┐
   │  1879   │                          │  1854   │   │  │
 • │ "Gdida" │                          │"Glaudin"│ steps
   │(new one)│                          │ (donor) │   │  │
   └─────────┘  clock                   └─────────┘   └──┘
         │     ←  ┌──────────────┐          │
         │ bells  │   Italian    │          │
         │        │    1735      │          │
         │        │ San Claurenc?│──────────┘
         │        │  "Mitquba"   │
         │        │   pierced    │         front wall
         └────────└──────────────┘──────────
```

(ex. 10) the right tower

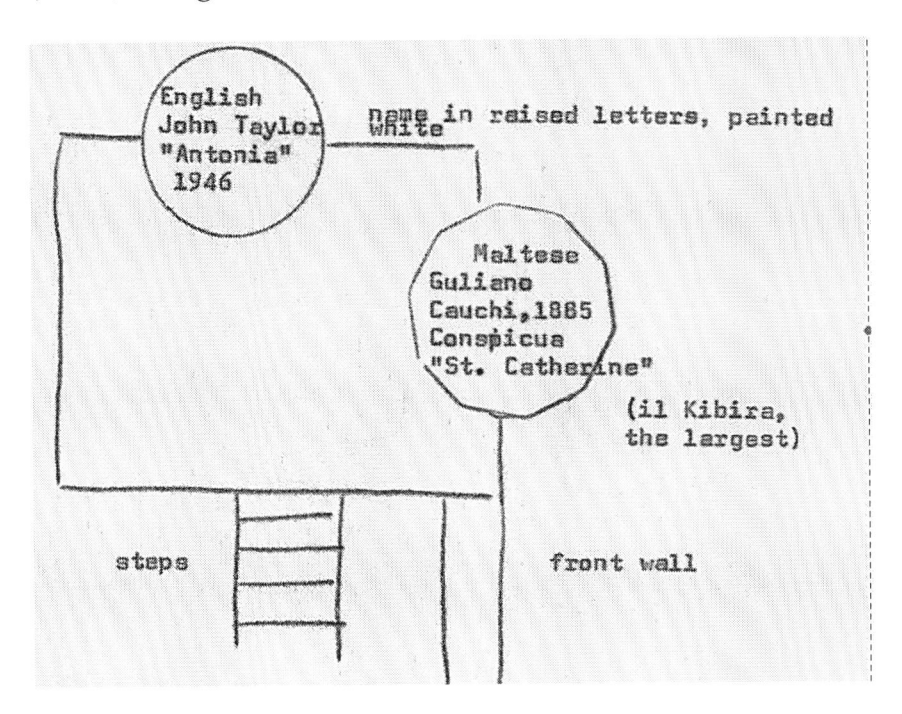

```
                 _____
                /English    \     name    in raised letters, painted
               | John Taylor |    white
               | "Antonia"   |
                \   1946    /
                 _____/
                          _____
                         / Maltese   \
                        / Guliano     \
                        | Cauchi, 1885 |
                        \ Conspicua   /
                         \"St. Catherine"/
                          _____/
                                           (il Kibira,
                                            the largest)

   steps    |=|                        front wall
            |=|
            |=|
            |=|
```

Mr. Grech took me across the roof, down a ladder and onto the roof of the left transept; which is evidently an older church. We examined the single bell there. It is dated 1816, and is called "Oratorio." (Maltese – Oratorja) Context: (are you ready for this?) Mr. Grech was talkative and full of information once I demonstrated a slight knowledge of the church bells. He insisted on running for a ladder and mounting every bell in order to get the date for me. Several times he stepped off the ladder entirely, and climbed around the rim of the bell like a fly.

Foto 9: Zejtun, ladder and Bells

He seemed unconcerned that the bells were suspended about 150-200 feet over the pavement. I was very concerned, especially when he climbed over the edge of Mitquba and circled it, his feet supported only by the narrow slope of the bell rim. He told me that the bell "Glaudin" was name after the family of a lady who paid for it. It had another name, but he didn't remember. Mitquba is the oldest bell and the largest in the left tower. "Mitquba" means "pierced," because the bell wasn't made with any rings at the top and they had had to bore holes and insert some U-bolts in order to hang it. He said "they didn't know to make the bells then."

On the right tower, "Antonia," the English bell and the newest one, seems especially elegant in its simple clear lines and white lettering. The largest bell (and it is really big) is St. Catherine, "Il kibra." It was made in Cospicue (Bormia) Malta, by Guiliano Cauchi in 1885.

I was able to ask Mr. Grech many questions about the bell, which he answered eagerly. Just try to keep your presence of mind on a church roof 200 feet I the air with the wind blowing you around. Also, try scribbling legibly in your notebook at the same time.

1. Trapassjoni (habar): Rung on "Glaudin" and "Oratorja".
   The bells alternate, first Glaudin, then Oatorja- ding-dong. There are 5 "ding-dongs" and then a pause, then 4 more sets. There are 25 double strokes. I did not get the time of day.
   This arrangement seems awkward, because Oratorja is some 100 feet away on the front of the small older church beside us.
2. Tal-Imwiet: 9 strokes on Il-Kibra. Rung at 9 PM in the summer, 8 PM in the winter
3. The bells at 8 AM, 12 Noon & sunset (Ave Maria) are rung on Il-Kibira.
4. "When Christ is dead" during Easter, i.e. during Friday and Saturday: they haul out a large wooden ratchet, not a wooden

bell, or rattle. It is stored in a large wooden shed over on the right wall. Maltese for ratchet; rota bissnen etc. Rattle= ceuqlajta etc. Mr. Grech said the shed was locked: see if you can get to it! He said they haul it out and put it over on the right tower.

5. The Pater Noster: They don't ring it at all. This was a sore spot with Mr. Grech, who elaborated at length. He said it was all the Bishop's fault (The Archbishop? I didn't catch his name). He said the bishop had been stationed in Burma or somewhere in the Far East among the savages who had no taste for finer things. When the Bishop came to Malta, he didn't like the Festal, he didn't like the bells. Also, some people complained, because they like to sleep. The Pater Noster was formerly rung ½ hour before the first mass at 3:30, 4 AM. To Mr. Grech, the bells are harmonious, comforting. He said he would awaken slightly in his sleep with the harmonious sound in his ears and turn over, comforted by the sound. But the Bishop didn't like them. At Zejtun, they gave a large amount of money to buy a gold crown, but the bishop wouldn't bless it. But, on the next day, he blessed a horse! He would bless a horse, but he wouldn't bless a golden crown the people had worked for. At the festal, he said, they would not fly his flag. I said, well, the bells are always here, but the bishop, someday he would leave. Mr. Grech liked that very much, and agreed. How Maltese of me!

On our way back from looking at Oratorja on the old church roof- most of our conversation was held in the little bell coop there with the wind blowing like mad- an old man appeared in the opening where a hole was cut for a ladder. Mr. Grech explained it was the Sexton, very old and almost blind. He didn't speak English. The old man was small, with swollen features. He was wearing a large cap with a bill on it, and he walked with his head down and with a shuffling gait. He seemed to know his way around the roof by memory. He talked to me and shook my hand. He said (Mr. Grech translated) he had been ringing the bells since he was 'that high'- 40 years.

Mr. Grech took me over to the cupola and spoke of it in admiration for the people who built it didn't have many tools such as cranes and derricks. The church was original built in 1720. A new roof had been added within his memory. He bounced up the side on the iron spoke ladder. I followed more slowly, but energetically enough. I didn't have time to enjoy my acrophobia. There was a door in the dome and he opened it and we looked down at the mass in progress, at the altar which was directly beneath. It was a moving sight. After we scrambled down, he pointed out some rounded pieces of masonry which had been intended for the dome but which had not been used and left on the wall. Towards the front of the church, he pointed out some repairs that had been made to the wall that had been damaged (cracked) by an earthquake. He said the stones had been loosened and were about to tumble down into the street below.

A small boy of about 14 accompanied the old sexton and followed us down the stairs. Mr. Grech said he was his brother's son. I took the opportunity to introduce myself, and thus learned the family name. I had been blinded by the sun on the roof, or rather my eyes had become so accustomed to the daylight that I had difficulty getting down the dark steps. The others seemed to have no trouble. At the bottom of the stairs, Mr. Grech showed me the 4 ropes that controlled the left hand bells. Evidently the two towers are rung independently. The large key was handed back to the old sexton, who seemed relieved to get it. Mr. Grech invited me back to hear the mota at 8:45 Thursday, for the Last Supper. He said to come about 8:15. He also said they would get me to ring the bells.

Some backups & tidbits: Mr. Grech pointed out the bell tower of the convent, which was visible from the roof of the older church. He said it was electric, made of tubular chimes. You couldn't ring them by hand- a Sister played them on a keyboard some times. The bells are set to play "Christus Vincit" on the hour. He said he chimes were French, "Picard" or "Bacard."

I asked him about the small bell fixed to the edge of the wall just to the left and in back of the dome. He said it was a signal bell, used to let the bell ringer know when to ring the bells for the benediction etc., because he bell ringer couldn't know otherwise. The bells went off several times while we were on the roof, and once Mr. Grech identified the benediction. Evidently some churches do announce the stages of the mass with the bells- the larger ones?

The young boy went out the door as I did, and passed me, saying "chao." I wondered if this was the boy Marcia had met at the cemetery, and I said to myself you ought to try to talk to him, also. As we passed my parked car, I offered to give him a ride, but he refused, a little nervously, I thought. I probably shouldn't have offered?

Wednesday, July 12

I rose rather later than I had planned. I was very tired from my crawl around Zejtun church, and also exhausted by having to type up the field notes of that day. Marcia and Norma drove me, via Marsaxloxx (where Marcia went in to see the seamstresses on Zejtun Road) and this time we went through Hamrun. Norma drove "grandmother" style at Marcia's suggestion, as Marcia was still queasy- in fact she had been feeling bad all the day before and had eaten light and easy.

At Mdina I got to work right away. The clock bells run on the same pattern as in Marsaxloxx and Zejtun, except two sizes of bells ring the quarter hour. The bells are unusual in that they seem to be tuned to each other. I noticed this as I was walking on my way to the cathedral museum and stopped to take a note.

In the museum, Father Azzopardi unlocked the archives for me and I sat down to continue the catalog of printed part books. I took the opportunity to mention I was very tired from the day before, when I was taken up on the roof of Zejtun church to see the bells. He remarked that we must soon set a date when he would show me the bells as he had promised. I think this is a typical example of stringing me out until the gets what he wants out of me, which is an article to the greater glory of the Mdina library. I also think it is a good example of stringing him out with an oblique approach; working on the Ms in order to get to the bells. Although I had not begun work on the bells, nor decided up on a project, this is the way it turned out.

I also mentioned I would like to talk to the sexton, to find out how the bells are rung. This brought a negative response from Father Azzopardi. He frowned, and said, I think that the sexton has ruined the bells. Or, he said the bells here are ruined. There used to be an old system of ringing all the bells together to call the whole island. Now, ropes have been attached to the bells, and they are rung from downstairs; I assume his is referring to a Mota, which is most effectively rung from the tower. He also said there were two new bells, about 28 years old, and that he had the documents there in the archives.

Father Azzopardi wanted to get the mess out of the archive study, as there was a meeting coming up next Monday. He said I might better come back tomorrow, Thursday 13th in the afternoon.

I went out of Mdina and had a coke and a candy bar at the small restaurant outside the parking lot, and wandered down to the benches. Marcia and Norma zipped right by me and stopped up the street. We returned via Hamrun again. The girls said they had had a flat tire when they were coming back through Hamrun or Attard, and that two very nice men from a truck had stopped and changed the tire for them. They had taken the car to Mr. Fenech, who as not particularly pleased, because the left front tire had been bruised and was ruined. He replaced the tire and washed the car.

This afternoon, I decided to go over to B'buga. After taking a picture of the front of the church, I walked around the right side, looking for the parish priest's house. The church at B'buga is very large and new. The style of architecture is more modern and austerely handsome. The bells and clock are located in a tall belfry to the right of the right tower. The stone lacks the gray, weathered appearance of most Maltese churches and the pinkish-yellow makes it appear brighter. The round dome in red and white, characteristic of most large Maltese churches was missing.

I located the Priest's house in the right hand projection of the church itself by the coat of arms with three fish and a wide brimmed hat. I was met at the door by a very pretty young girl. There were two curtained doors to either side of the central hall, as seems to be usual in Priest's houses. I was seated momentarily in the right hand room. It contained a large wooden table- a dining table I believe, - at TV set, a large box of Maltese "Smoker's Delight" cigarettes and a dark chest- the type in which you keep your china- against the wall opposite the door. Two framed pictures were set on top of the cabinet- I guess you can call it- a marriage photo, and a picture of two smiling children. It struck me odd until I remembered that in Malta, priests live with their families and that I was in fact seated in a family dining room. The girl must have been a relative.

In a minute, the girl returned to tell me I could go in now (cheap labor to get your relatives to serve you). I went into the room opposite the hall through a curtained doorway and found a small, darkly tanned man seated at a desk. He was wearing a black shirt and collar, and a pair of black trousers with a tan belt- quite a change from the usual gown that most priests wear. His features were sharp- long thin nose. He was about 45 or 50, and his hair was thinning but not gray. He wore plastic rimmed glasses. His manner was very astute and business like. He rose as I greeted him and explained my mission. He did not introduce himself. He said, yes, he could tell me about the bells, but (gesturing to the desk) he had much work right then, perhaps I could return? I said fine, what time, or could he direct me to someone else who could give me the information I wanted? He didn't seem to want to set a time for my return or tell me who to talk to. I think here is where the polite but firm policy paid off. He finally asked what I wanted to know and went over to haul out a large volume of correspondence. He explained that the bells were new, having been installed in July of 1969, and that he had two years of letters and specifications I could examine, and then he carefully kept the volume to himself and gave me some dimensions and statistics. He seemed to warm up a bit as I asked him some questions about the various bells and their ringing. He said the bells are not electric, but they are rung by hand, because the tone is better that way.

All in all, this parish priest seemed to know more about the bells than any other I have talked to, not only about the physical qualities of the bells themselves, but about the names and the number of strokes used. This is partially because he was instrumental in buying and installing the bells, I think, but he also seemed to appreciate them and reacted favorably to my comments about their quality. And they are truly beautiful bells, clear and sharp in the higher register, as I noticed from the few times they rung while I was there- it was about 5:00 PM. He asked if I like the bells, and I said they were harmonious, but I thought some people did not like them. He smiled and said that you couldn't please everybody.

This man was most astute. He was not giving anything away. Earlier I remarked that the bells must have cost a lot of money. He only agreed.

The following is a summary:

Name	Maltese Name	Pitch	Diameter	Weight
1. St. Peter	Il-Kbir (large)	C	59"	4,972
2. Our Lady of Sorrows	It-Tghin (2nd)	E	47"	2,433
3. St. Joseph	It-Tielet (3rd)	G	39"	1,485
4. St. Paul, Apostle	Ir-Raba (4th)	A	35"	1,056
5. St. Catherine, Virgin & Martyr	Iz-Zghira (smallest)	C	29"	616

(The parish priest made some reference to the bells being in minor, but the E, the third of the cluster, was just E and not Eb. Was he talking about color or tone?)

Funeral bell: No. 4, for its sober one. Tone is important in the selection of bells for particular occasions.

Tal-Imwiet: 8PM No. 2, 9 strokes

Pater Noster: 4:45, 6 strokes on No. 5, "not to make so much noise"

Thursday for the last supper: Mota of Thursday=Mota Tal-Hamis

Friday, for death of Christ: Mota of 3 o'clock

Ave Maria, at sunset

Maker, Petit & Fritsen, (Holland) Aarle Rixtel.

The clock rings V and III.

Foto 10: Birzebbuga Church

I also remember he (the parish priest) made some remark that I could find a lot of information on the bells in America, but I didn't budge.

I didn't get as much as I wanted from this priest, I could have, for example, asked the bell and strokes for the Ave Maria. But as the interview had gone well up to that point, I decided to take the better part of valor and not to impose on him longer. I thanked him and shook hands and left. On my way back I took a picture of the belfry, and stepped into the things in the front of the church and watched the altar from the two sides and the back. The interior looked a little Mozarabic, with interior arches and flat columns along the sides. The interior was well lighted from the sunlight coming through the narrow window. The altar was basking in the sun from an opening above. Everything was spacious and pinkish tan. Some varnished wooden pews, movable with slats in the back were placed up front. They were more like long, benches and looked very comfortable. I didn't see a bowl of holy water (so I didn't pollute it with my Protestant fingers).

On my way back to Hal T. I stopped at Tony's Aviator Bar in Marsaxloxx to pick up a case of beer. There were about six Inglese in the bar, three young pretty girls, tanned and wearing beach clothes, an older, blonde woman with a small child and two short-clad hairy young men, athletic and tanned. I presumed they were from the Oceanographic vessel down on the quay. One of the girls, who was sitting to the left of the bar, was quite pretty with shoulder length raven black hair and bright blue eyes. I tried not to stare. She was about 27 or 30, and her teeth were pearl white. One of the other girls was sitting to the right of the door, down front. She was also well tanned, but had rather sharp features. Through a slit in her beach clothes, I saw she was wearing a bikini. The other girl facing her was a blonde, but I couldn't see her very well. Ah well.

I toyed for a moment on the way home of hitting Zabbar, but decided against getting too much grist in my mill.

Later, Norma called me out into the garden this evening to hear the bells from Zejtun ringing. The started at 8:15PM and rang for about 5 minutes. The bells were ringing a fast alternation between a major 2nd and a minor 2nd, like dee-da-dah-da-dee-da-dah-da. The half step was like an auxiliary tone.

Analysis time. Several things now point to a rift between progressives and conservatives shaping up in Malta, of which the bells may be one facet.

Progressives = several strata

1. The young
2. Educated, higher class
3. Pro-modernity, against Maltese backwardness
4. The liberal wing of the church who want to "modernize" and "update"

Conservatives

1. The old
2. Country folk
3. Malta for the Maltese
4. The traditionalist wing of the church

The controversy seems at surface to circle around the noise of the bells, and the fireworks (see clipping Malta Times, July 12).

Political element, i.e., what do the Malta Laborites think about the bells, the fireworks? (See Johnny S's story about the ringing of the bells during political rallies. Projection: could be split within politics as within church.) However, I have no information that any priests (except the Archbishop) are anti-bells, although- Father Delicata did not want to spend money on fireworks in Marsaxloxx. I think I it is a safe bet that there is a liberal-conservative division in the Maltese church. Also, I think you would get mixed opinions among MLP members (actively political) as to the fireworks and bells, according to how far alienation has set in.

So, in effect, there might be a controversy that cut across the boundaries of politics and religion. Boissevian mentioned a division of Band Clubs by politics. How to get at it? Cull notes for evidence.

I remember some remarks that I do not believe I put in the notes. One was made by an Englishman, "Max," at Joan Grundy's house next door. There was that odd couple, older man and woman (soused) who admired my Celtic features (!). The party was on June 18th, the Sunday the village festival started. The church bells had gone off at 5 AM and woke everyone up. I remember this well, as I was asleep near an open window. I almost jumped out of it (!).

Max complained about "the bloody bells and the Quasimodo who rings them". (Belief that all bell ringers are a little off?). Remark about the nutty boy who rang them? Think this is the strange fellow I saw at the boat house yesterday, the one Norma says steals the garbage before the chap who steals the garbage before the garbage truck comes. I also remember a remark that Lena G. made that she didn't like the bells, even though she (according to her sister Mary) is an ardent church-goer?

How could I elicit some evidence? Start some conversations: "Suppose they stopped the bells (fireworks), what would happen then?"

"I really like the bells, but I understand some people don't like them".

"Oh, listen to the bells, I think they are a bloody nuisance".

Bait, bait, bait. In a fisherman's village, you might catch something? Maybe not: Norma's remark about Marsaxloxx being an atypical village.

Who to ask? Marcia's suggestions: drop in at the MLP bar. Drop in to a store when the bells go off.

People: Johnny S. Mary and Lena G
Joe Attard   Joan Grundy
France Geatt   The Scotts, any Inglesi
Johnny M.   The boys at Rediffusion
Carminu B.   Mr. Grech

Bait: "I was over to X and they took me up on the church and showed me the bells." Remember how this worked this morning?

Marsaxloxx, Zejtun, B'buga, are seemingly disobeying a directive about ringing the Pater Noster before 6AM. See if you can get copy of this directive: probably every church has it.

Thursday, July 13:

Morning; I got up around 8:30, I think, a little irked by traffic in front of the house that had awakened me, and the fly that returned to haunt me by lighting on my nose every time I managed to doze back off.

Marcia had reviewed my notes together with Norma Tuesday night and offered some criticisms, towit, be more specific, detailed, be careful to describe colors (avoid black and white-isms), be more analytic and include our mental processes, pick your nits and especially be self-critical, and include your "mea culpas".

Last night, Marcia and I had a long session about the alternatives left open to me at this date, i.e. what to focus upon. Three studies suggested themselves: 1), in-depth study of bell ringers and sextons who ring bells, concepts, aesthetics, training recruitment, why do people say they are odd, etc. This is perhaps too time consuming in view of the Maltese dislike of personal questions, it would take a long time. 2), a description/ comparison of bells and bell patters in Malta- this I could probably do by hitting 3-4 more churches with talkative bell ringers. Marcia tended to think this was "Bb" ("ordinary"} and not ethnomusicology. 3), A study of the traditionalist-modernist rift as suggested by the controversy over the Pater Noster and the fireworks. This was really hot stuff, according to Marcia. Norma was asked about the Bb study As usual she managed to get my back up. She said: "do you really want to get out of the library" and left. Earlier, there was some talk of my wanting to go to Gozo for the Victoria festal, in which the band club had declined to participate because the question of their titular saint being bashed off the calendar had not been resolved. Posters had been pasted on the churches and the priests had refused to say Mass. Earlier, they had locked the priests out of their churches for an extended period, several weeks. This occurred several years ago. At present, it is unclear to me just why I should want to bop off to Gozo; it seemed to be expected of me. I was very pissed off at Norma and I reacted negatively all morning today, i.e. not speaking, shutting my door. Perhaps Norma did not mean it the way I took it, but it upset me.

Thursday, July 12

This morning, (Thursday) I stayed home to review my notes and take stock. Marcia and Norma went off to doodle in Valletta. About 11:30 I gathered up my stuff (my camera, notebook, pipe, etc. in my bag) and walked off down to St. Thomas Bay.

The road is called Ramla Road. There is an old church (1823) right at the corner, a little way from Hal-Tmiem. I passed by the usual block-style farmhouses and a few interesting pill-box type fortifications which had been converted into dwellings. I passed on defaced Knights of Malta mileposts. Turning off Ramla Road, which leads to Marsaskala, I noticed a shrine in which had been defaced with the letters "LP" (Labor Party). The sign pointing to Zejtun in the opposite direction had been neatly crossed out with white paint. The LP letters were painted in blue on the grey of the shine.

The road to St. Thomas Bay led downwards, past an uncompleted apartment development. The settlement itself consisted mainly of ramshackle dwellings, not a few of which were put together from sheet tin, and, I believe, scrap metal from old buses.

(ex. 10)

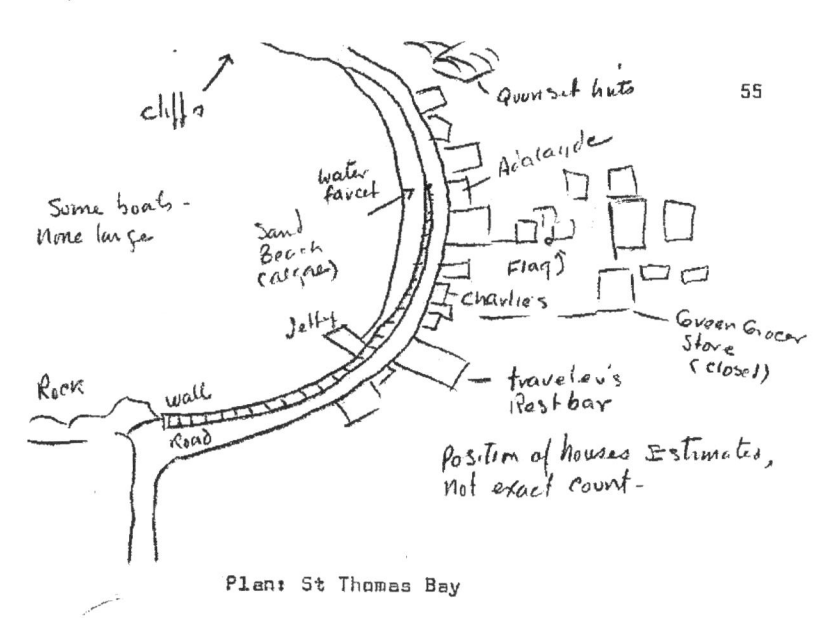

Sketch map labeled "Plan: St Thomas Bay" showing: cliffs, Quonset huts, Adalaude, water faucet, Sand Beach (coarse), Some boats - none large, Jetty, Flags, Charlies, Green Grocer Store (closed), Rock, wall, Road, traveler's Rest bar. Note: "Position of houses Estimated, not exact count."

All in all, the settlement was not picturesque at all, but rather jumbled together. Walking down the road, my curiosity was aroused by a flag flying a little back from the beach. It was Japanese; white with a red ball in the middle. As I walked down the sandy road, I passed some young boys fishing and playing around. The wind was quite strong, and it blew the sand in my eyes. I passed some cute little girls on the way back from the store with some bottles slung in a net basket between them, and one of them said "hello" to me, and I said "hello" back. I walked down the road to the end of the rock wall, which became progressively lower and more crumbly. As I paused to rest, a young boy turned on a water faucet and tried to spray his companion, an older boy, with it. I wondered if the water was carried by the metal pipe of about 3" diameter which I had noticed paralleling the left side of Ramla Road all the way down from Fejn Il-Hwienet ("The Place (near) the stores"), which seems to be a general designation for the crossroads up the street from Hal-Tmiem. I passed three bars, "Traveler's Rest," "Charlie's," and "Adalyade Bar." I walked back past the Adalyade Bar (see map) and discovered a short ally leading into a large square place which contained a store, the "Green Grocers" at the far end to the right. The Japanese flag was attached to a pole in front of a low dwelling with a small-enclosed space in front, which contained several tables. Three women were sitting at the front table, eyeing me suspiciously and studiously ignoring me. Well, they were eyeing me out of the corner of their eyes. Is that better? There were some advertisements pasted on the left hand wall. I supposed it was a bar or restaurant, but it bore no sign. I started to go over and ask about the flag, but decided it would be too bold. Instead, I went back to Charlie's bar and got a beer, which I really didn't want because my bladder was full and my prostate was getting sore as it sometimes does.

There were two lumpy men in the small bar. The man behind the counter was thin, wizened by the sun and hadn't shaved for a day or so. I bought a Hopleaf and cooled it at a nearby table. There were only two tables besides the bar, and the storage room at the rear was leaking empty bottles out its door and into the bar. In the center of the floor, a bitch was standing, placidly suckling three pups, which were making loud suckling noises. No one paid any attention to the dogs. Most of the conversation at the bar centered about counting money. Several people came in, including two children, a boy and a girl, to exchange empties. The boy was dressed in shirt and short pants (yellow and blue, respectively) and was wearing shoes and socks, and glasses. I wondered if he was English, but he spoke in Maltese.

Eventually, the bar was empty except for the bar tender and myself, and we struck up a conversation about the strong wind and the fishermen, who were not going out today because of it. I finally asked him about the flag, but he didn't understand until I drew him a picture. He said the people were Maltese, not Japanese, and that they flew many flags, English, German, etc. I asked if it was because of the football (soccer) teams, but he saw no connection.

The Maltese seem to be fond of putting out flags. The roundabout in front of King's Gate at Valletta is decorated with the flags of many nations, and so is the street leading to the gate. On the road to Marsaxloxx from Hal-Tmiem (i.e. the Delamara Road), you can see a Swiss flag and Norwegian flag flying from a villa on the right. Marcia says there is actually a Swiss lady living on the top floor, and that Finn W. might have given the other flag to the occupants. There is a shop in Hamrun on the main road next to Barclay's Bank that actually makes flags.

Having solved this riddle, I finished my beer and made my way home again. One the way up to Ramla Road, I passed the small boy with glasses I had seen in the bar. He was standing in a doorway with his mother (perhaps), and some other small children. He said "Hello" in English and the other children chimed in, with some amusement. Marcia says it is a big thing to practice your English on a real live Inglese. I passed two young girls sitting on the knobby stone fence opposite the shrine, and I noticed a lonely knobby little girl in a blue-white school uniform with a book case seated on a stone against the opposite wall, waiting for a bus; very Norman Rockwell-ish.

As I was nearing Hal-Tmiem, a young man in a white Anglia stopped and offered me a ride. As it was almost 1 PM by then, I accepted. He was dressed in slacks and silk shirt with brown check patterns, and wearing metal-rimmed glasses- urban style, the large square-ish sunglass type frame with is popular here. He dropped me off at the intersection. We did not have time to strike up a conversation. I thanked him and went back to the house thru the garage. The car was there. I washed off, and lay down for half an hour, then fixed a sandwich and then took off for Mdina at 2 PM.

I arrived at Mdina via Hamrun about 2:30. As I approached the cathedral, I paused to take down the time bells, and I did this several times in the Archive study room as I worked. I think the time bells for the quarter hour are a major 7th apart, and the hour bell an octave below the highest tone, three tones in all. For the second quarter, I am not still sure. I think the beginning tone varies. At 2:45, the bells were ascending. I am sure about 3 PM: Major 7th (down), major 7th, major 2nd. I am annoyed that I cannot recall a simple bell pattern and its intervals.

In the archives, I completed the cataloging of the printed part books and managed to pump Father Azzopardi some about the bells. He is acting very canny. Actually, he wants someone to do a book on (another) Father Azzopardi whose manuscript they have, about 200 works in all. I agreed to return Monday at 11, when he would show me the bells, and when I would look at the (other) Azzopardi, as payment.

Father Azzopardi took out an old catalogue and read me off the names of the bells, only he read them so fast and got them so confused I will have to check them again. No use in getting him mad at me because I am so slow and he speaks such rapid English.

For what it's worth, there are 2 bells for the clock, which dates from 1884. The bells are dated 1634 and 1398. There are 4 other bells. Anna Maria (date unknown) Paula, Messina 1728; Patronela (he said was dedicated to St. Paul); Peter, Venice 1370 and another bell dated 1616, with no reference to names.

I asked Father Azzopardi about the Archbishop's edict. He said it occurred 3-4 years ago and admitted to having the circular, but it was in Maltese. He might haul it out, but he doesn't want to. He also said that the smaller villages rang the Pater Noster before 6, as it was more meaningful and functional in the villages than in the cities. He also asked me not to publish that the villages were disobeying the edict, and I agreed. Rats! It is possible that everyone, i.e. church officials, are quite aware that the edict is being ignored, but that they are afraid to enforce it rigidly.

Father Azzopardi said the bells at Mdina were rung by hand for feasts, but it is too far to climb to ring by hand every day. Actually, the church in Mdina doesn't seem any larger than Zejtun, only richer. However, it may be that it is especially difficult to get at the bells. I think Father Azzopardi said the bell ringer had "ruined" the bells, because he doesn't want to take the trouble to ring them upstairs, perhaps. Because they had ropes attached recently. Perhaps he is getting too old to climb stairs? Or, since this is the head church in Malta, the Archbishop felt safe in restricting the use of the bells here? You can't ring the bells fast enough for the mota by rope- can't get a double stroke, only a single one. How do they ring the mota in B'buga, from that narrow belfry with 5 bells in it? Have they given it up there, too?

Father Azzopardi has "the most beautiful church" in a small village outside Mdina- didn't catch the name. He said there are three bells there, one by Guliano Cauchi, the Maltese bell maker. He said the "tongue" i.e. the clapper, on one bell had rusted and been taken down and then lost. He wondered who in Malta might make another. I said I would check, intending to ask Mr. Grech that evening. Actually, I forgot, but it will make an excellent excuse to look him up again. Also, this would be another good question for other bell ringers. I saw the name "Grech" painted in the Marsaxloxx tower over Victoria. Perhaps Grech works on bells. I do know that a bell ringer for Zejtun rings the Marsaxloxx bells, but I didn't ascertain if it was Mr. Grech. I asked indirectly, but got no response. Perhaps there is a "specialist" bell repairer in Malta. Wow, would he have the dope!

I returned to Hal-Tmiem after a snack in the outdoor restaurant- coke and a candy bar. At 8 PM I packed up the tape recorder and drove to Zejtun to record the bells. I arrived just exactly at 8:15. Mr. Grech was waiting for me with some other people, seemed relieved I had arrived. We went up the stairs immediately. I gathered I was just in the nick of time and that they had just about decided to go on up anyway, without me. One of the young men said "you got here right on the dot."

There were eight people present. Mr. Grech, his nephew, two smaller boys, an older man, a chubby boy with sandy blond hair of about 19, a slender boy with dark hair and sideburns and one other boy whose visage I cannot remember. I sat up the tape recorder in the middle of the roof next to the front wall, with everyone gathered around. I was amazed at how much they know about tape recorders and at the perceptive questions they asked. As I took out the Beyer microphone, Grech's nephew sucked in his breath (evil eye?). We discussed the possibility of recording from the center of the roof, but everyone agreed it was too windy there. I learned that a man from the rediffusion had recorded the bells from there once. As the time neared 8:30, the people began dispersing to their various posts, seemingly without any direction. Mr. Grech explained that he sent the two smaller boys off to ring Oratorio on the smaller church beside them, because they were little and could scramble down the ladder to the roof next door. When Marcia and Norma had a flat in Hamrun, two men and a boy came and helped them change the tire. They said the two men let the small boy do most of the work until he could do no more and then took over. Marcia remarked she thought it was an excellent way to train the children.

Mr. Grech explained the order of ringing. He seemed pleased I know the names of the bells (I had memorized the names and positions). 1, Oratorio, 2, Gdida, 3, Mitquba, 4, Antonia, 5, Kbira.

He said they did not use the smallest, Ruzarja, because of the tone. I didn't get why Glaudin, the other bell, was not used.

The mota was the usual single stroke into a double stroke by accelerando, one bell at a time. I did not think it was done as smoothly as at Marsaxloxx. Mr. Grech directed the beginning of the bells, one by one. First, the clock stuck 8:30, and Oratorio began ringing at once. The first stroke entries were quite dramatic. The ringers got the heavy clappers swinging back and forth before they began. Grech's nephew was on Gdida, the older man on Mitquba. On the other tower, the boy I cannot remember, was on Antonia, and the light haired chubby boy rang Kbira. The dark slender boy stood on the roof with me. Mr. Grech paced back and forth checking his watch. Several times he put his fingers in his ears. The mota lasted 15 minutes precisely. Mr. Grech cued the stop and all the bells stopped at once. Almost immediately, the clock rang 8:15. They all came back to me at once, and I replayed the tape through the loud speaker. Mr. Grech was ecstatic. He kept saying "Jesus Christ." He told me several times this was the best recording he had ever heard of the bells. Evidently, then, several people have recorded the bells. He said once someone came with a small recorder, but it wasn't any good. They were so taken with the fidelity of the recording and the excellence of the Swiss made Nagra tape deck that I could not steer the conversation in any other direction. I told the dark slender boy (he was about 17) that I liked the bells because they made little melodies. He understood what I meant.

Mr. Grech explained they were going to ring the Tal-Imwiet at 9, and then they had to leave, as the church was being closed. I threaded a new reel on the recorder, but the automatic record interfered too much with the 6 strokes made on Kbira to be worth anything. They helped me gather up my stuff and we went back down the stairs again. One the way down, the slender boy pointed out the door to the organ loft. There were two metal doors, one halfway down and one at the bottom. Mr. Grech was careful to lock both with a large key. At the landing there was more conversation, mainly about the possibility of having the Rediffusion broadcast the recording I had just made over a program called "Wirt Artna". I had to borrow a pencil from the older man as I had chunked everything, pen included, into the handbag.

I asked about the Friday 3 PM ringing. Mr. Grech said it was not a mota, but a type of melody rung from downstairs. He said he would not be here, but I could come and record from in front of the church. Another man was waiting at the bottom of the stairs, a balding, older type of person. Mr. Grech said he was another Sexton.

I walked to the parking lot with Grech's nephew and the slender boy, talking about the Rediffusion, the "radio" station that they have piped into a metal horn suspended on a pole in the church yard. It sounds all the time. As we passed a building on the other side of the street which had some initials in red metal figures attached to the front, the slender boy asked me if I knew what it was, and said something complicated in Maltese, He asked Grech's nephew what it meant, and the little Grech said it was the Teenager's Club, "for virgins," the other added, and we laughed.

Some backups. On the way to Zejtun that evening I passed behind the old cemetery church, San Girgor. Over to the left, a slender man with a blue silk shirt and striped bell bottomed trousers was backing up another older man with baggy trousers against the wall. They were embracing, and the younger man had his left leg raised over the hip of the other man. Marcia had noticed them on her way back from Zejtun- she had gone to Luqa airport to mail letters about hotel reservations in London. She thought it was a man and a chubby girl. They had disappeared by the time I drove back. This is the place where the dumpy old man in vest and cap comes out to wave a paper or something when I pass by, sometimes.

Mary Grech, our former housemaid, said her aunt was a nun, and that she was always trying to get her and Lena interested in joining up. Mary said she hoped the nun would not pray for her to become one of them (as the aunt had said she was), because the Lord might hear and come for her.

The time sense of Maltese must be very well tuned and ingrained. For example, getting there early for an appointment. How does it tie in with bells? Did the Archbishop's edict mess up their time- aesthetic? Is there such a thing as a time aesthetic among the Maltese? That's an odd thought. Time values in relation to the bells, ones that reinforce them?

Hang out in Zejtun until you meet some of those boys?

The de-da-dah-da bell pattern I had noticed in the garden at Hal-Tmiem at 8:5 comes from the convent, not Zejtun. I heard them on the Zejtun church roof this evening again, just before the clock went off. Mr. Grech said they had to do with something like "40 hours."

The Angelus rang just as we arrived on the roof this evening. It contained several pitches, but did not get. It was rung downstairs. Mr. Grech said it was the sunset bell. The 9 PM bell I heard at Marsaxlokk on Thursday, July 6th (2 strokes on Carmena?) may have been the sunset bell. This occurred the evening I was stood up by Joe Attard.

Things to check:

1. Who likes bells, who doesn't, why?
2. Do people really recognize the bells by name?
3. Who does and who doesn't?

Friday, July 14th

Figuring and field notes in the morning; Marcia and Norma go to dressmakers for a fitting. At 2:45m we left to go and pay Mr. Fenech his weekly rent on the car, - £11- and to check the Rediffusion and to pick up some groceries and supplies. We paused in Zejtun so I could hear the Friday bell for the Death of Jesus. We parked over near the band club and went to the bench in front of the church. As I was walking over, four lumpy old men who had been sitting on the benches to the right of the church in front of the busses got up and ambled into the church, two to the right entrance and two to the left. They were dressed in the common rig, light shirt with rolled up sleeves, baggy trousers, sandals an caps.

I guessed that they were the sextons or people who were going to ring the bells.

The Friday 3 PM ringing goes like this:

(ex. 12)

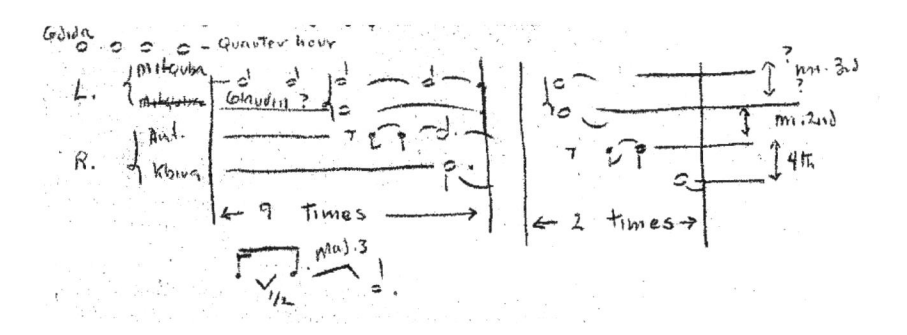

After the ringing was finished, I went over to look into the church to see if I could corner someone, but they had all left. The old sexton whom I had met on the roof passed me, but he didn't see good and he probably didn't notice me. Besides, he doesn't speak English. Back at the car, Norma, who had gone to inspect the stalagmite critically positioned in the middle of the crossroads to hold up the traffic, told us the inscription promised anyone who said a credo in front of it a hundred years off in purgatory. Earlier, she had properly identified one of the ringing bells as having a crack in it! It was the bell called "mit Uba" ("with a hole"). She has a fantastic ear (and I told her so!).

After paying Mr. Fenech, we drove to the Rediffusion in Gwatdamagga. I went to the TV station, while Marcia and Norma went in the Rediffusion. We agreed to meet in the cafeteria there. I went into the TV and found Joe (Verraro? Valleck?) from Zabbar, the attendant who led me in said.) Joe was riding the gain for a TV program visible on the monitors. Two other people were at the console. After they finished, I apologized for breaking in unannounced and explained that I wanted a dub of the seratta we had seen there. Joe asked if I wanted any other material, bells perhaps. It turns out that Rediffusion has recordings of all the bells in the Malta churches, which are sent off to the radio stations in America and Australia for nostalgia. He also said they had a sound catalogue of fireworks, "sounds like Vietnam to you eh?"-I I thought this was a very revealing remark- and carriages and boat oars. He said he would do the dubbing for me, but he was busy and didn't know when he could get to it. I asked if I should get someone in the other station to do it, but he insisted and so I left him three rolls of audio tape. We had some parallel conversation about taking the tapes back to America and playing them on 60 cycle equipment. He said the machines here in Malta ran on 50 cycles. Surely (I said) 7.5 ips was the same everywhere? (Check at the local radio stations first- it may save you scads of trouble and get you all kinds of contacts.)

I found Marcia and Norma in the cafeteria right away. They had drawn a complete blank as the people they wanted to see kept early hours only, 8 to 12 or something like that. We drove to Sliema and dropped Marcia off at the supermarket. Norma and I went around the corner to the large hotel, the pre-Luna, but only located the Gozo ferry schedule in a booklet we found next door in another smaller hotel. We picked Marcia up and rove to Valletta for some film and tobacco, then drove home.

Saturday, July

This morning, Marcia and Norma went off to check on airline tickets and to mail some translations back marked "educational material." Norma got very angry and threw a pen at me. She borrowed it while attempting to write her address on one of the envelopes. She thought her pen was running out of ink. As she handed it back, I said, "That's all right, you keep it." I intended it as a joke, because I had been kidding Marcia about borrowing a pen from me about 6 weeks ago, then sticking it in her mouth and walking off with it. Marcia said Norma was the real pen gatherer. But Norma said "I wouldn't think of it" and threw the pen at me and stomped off to get her own pen. She was really angry. Marcia said "oh, oh, off in a snit." I felt very bad that Norma was mad, but I couldn't get angry with her. Am I overly possessive about things that are mine, do I not share enough with others? I must give this some thought.

After they had left, I went up on the sunroof and poured over Marcia's field notes for references to time. I decided there were at least 8 major categories of time:

1. Punctuality
2. Tempo
3. Regularity, or periodicity

4. Elapsed times
5. Repetition
6. Numbers and time
7. Social time
8. Order (sequence)

Norma and Marcia returned about 1:30. The airline tickets were not ready. They had visited someone for advice about how to act- what was expected of us- in relation to the impending death of Paula Scicluna's mother. They returned with some proverbs similar to "a friend in need," etc. Norma acted normally, didn't seem mad anymore, and spoke to me.

Around 7PM, I went for a walk, and took the road back to Zejtun and turned off on the Wied Iz Ziju Road, the "valley of the olive-leaved blackthorn." I stopped to look at the freshly painted church just around the corner. It is very small, with a single bell over the door. The bell clapper had some fabric tied over it. The walls had been painted bright yellow. There was a Maltese cross over the door, with the date 1537. It must have been one of the first churches in this area.

As I continued up the road, I noticed that some of the stones in the rock wall had been painted white, in addition to the RTO number painted on the stones in small red letters. At the top of a hill I came upon a grand mansion called "Il-Continju." It had broken glass cemented to the top of the high wall. Over the hill a way, I came to a large quarry. I walked to the edge, and then walked back to the house. At home, I lay down for a short rest.

About 8 o'clock, I heard the sound of a motorbike pull up outside. We had been expecting Johnny to call all day with news of Paula's Mother. I met him at the door. He looked tired and worried. Marcia came to the door in her swimsuit and together we pulled him in to the living room and plunked a drink in front of him. Norma was back working in the field. It was hot and the wind had been blowing sand in Jonny's eyes. Marcia tactfully brought up the subject of Paula's mother. We learned that she had been taken back to her home in Qrendi. At the hospital, they said they could do no more for her. Johnny said she had had an operation on her stomach, and the doctor (Professor, he said) told them she would be lucky if she lived a year.

Paula and Mary and Paula's brother were still there. Johnny had just returned.

Just before I had to leave, Marcia told Johnny about the thing in Gozo (the posters in the church, the priest refusing to say mass, the band refusing to play, etc.). Johnny hadn't heard about it. He said you wouldn't learn of these things form the Malta Times. I took the opportunity while Marcia was out (she ran into the bedroom to change into a dress) to ask Johnny about the curious face hair I had seen on several Maltese near the eyes on the cheekbone. I had guessed it denoted membership in some kind of religious fraternity, as I had seen hair like this on the Monsignor I had been introduced to by Father Azzopardi in Mdina.

But Johnny said no, that he had hair like that and it is too close to the bone to shave, you have to cut it off with scissors. Evidently some people didn't bother. I haven't been going around looking at girl's arm pits, but the few I do recall were hairy. Also, it seemed to me that girl's legs there were probably only shaved about once a month. I didn't ask and I'm glad I didn't.

I left to meet Joe Attard as per our previous arrangement. I got to Marsaxlokk at 8:45- proper Maltese meeting time, but Joe wasn't there. I hung around for a while, then walked down the quay and returned just as the clock was striking. No Joe. I sat down and looked at the boats for a while. In a minute, I saw Joe with a bicycle and rolled up towel and swimsuit arguing with someone in front of Tony's bar. I walked over, and he said "OK, just a minute, huh?" I saw that Mr. Gatt had returned to his usual chair a little way down from the parish priest's house (he lives up on St. Catherine Street. Why does he sit there?) He had just returned from ringing something at 9 PM- I had noticed this last Saturday. He had rung 5 groups of 4. I greeted him and sat on the sidewalk, waiting for Joe, who had obviously gone home to dispose of his bike. The sexton was very embarrassed, I think. I quickly exhausted my supply of Maltese greetings. In a minute, Joe came back up, said we could go now. The sexton went back to lock the door and joined us in the car. Joe apologized for being 6 minutes late. Joe is the only Maltese I have made appointments with who is consistently late.

As we drove past the Tas-silg Monastery Church, Joe said they were going to celebrate the feast there tomorrow. The church building had been outline with electric light bulbs.

Back at Hal-Tmiem, we went through the living room and into the hall, at Norma's suggestion- she was up and she and Marcia were still talking to Johnny. On the way over, Joe had asked if Johnny M. would be there. I explained that, no, but another Johnny is there, Scicluna form Zabbar, a singer. The sexton giggled. They must think we are running an information factory. Also, Joe told me that Johnny's sister (Johnny Maniscalco) was getting married tomorrow and I asked him if it wasn't' his brother instead. Joe laughed and said he had made a mistake. Yes, it was Johnny's brother.

In the hall I plunked some drinks down and started to ask some questions. But Joe got confused and wanted to start where we had left off the week before, where ever that was. I gave in and pulled out the papers I had been writing on then, just to pretend. Joe wanted to conduct the interview! During the next 45 minutes, he and the sexton had prolonged arguments and discussions. All I got was the equivalent of "He say 'no.'" I could almost follow what the sexton was saying. He was reeling out information that Joe was discarding and condensing into what he thought I wanted him to say. The generation gap was apparent. Joe was rather impatient with the Sexton. Once while we were talking about the "Ta L-orazjona" bell, I tried to establish how many strokes and what grouping, and I was able to bypass Joe by holding up 4 fingers five times; to which the sexton grinned, and nodded, and repeated my gestures.

I guess I'm trying to say that Joe is a lousy translator, not his fault, but mine. He doesn't really know much about the bells, although he rings them occasionally. He did not remember the name of Marjia, the small bell. The Sexton was impressed that I had.

The "Ta L-orazjona" bell is a new ringing Joe had not mentioned. It was the bell I had heard at 9 PM. It was rung everyday on Marjia one hour before Tal-Imwiet. The strokes are 5 groups of 4. It is rung "for the Madonna" I heard the Sexton say. Joe said it "was to pray for Mary."

Next, I tried to find out if there were people who repaired bells in Malta- evidently not. If a bell is damaged, they send it to England (and Italy, I heard the sexton say, but Joe didn't mention this). I told them about Father Azzopardi's problem with the "bell tongue", and learned there is an iron foundry at Naxxar where metal work is sometimes done.

Next, I said "suppose I am a bell ringer, and something happens and I don't get to ring some bell or other on time. Would I ring it anyway, or what would happen?" The sexton shook his head and said some bells had to be rung on time, particularly the 8 AM and the noon bells, because people set their watches and go to mass etc. It was unthinkable that these important bells would be rung late! Joe assured me Mr. Gatt was very conscientious and would not do such a thing. Mr. Gatt added if a bell were more than 5 minutes late, it should not be rung. Other bells were more flexible. For example, the Tal-Imwiet could be rung anywhere between 10 and 10:10.

The most tantalizing problem arose next. I described how in Zejtun they rung the Tal-Imwiet with six strokes instead of 12. Joe and the Sexton had a long conversation. I heard the sexton reel off "pa exampu's" and list towns. Joe said merely that the sexton was using the old system, and that other towns were using the new. I should have really bored in on this until I found out the difference between the two systems (if there are two systems). But I was getting pissed at Joe, and I suspected that I could not get him to translate more literally, because his English was poor, and because he didn't understand why I wanted to know. In fact, several times he said "why you want to know that?" Joe said at first the sexton in Zejtun liked to sleep, that's why he rung the Tal-Imwiet at 9 with only 6 strokes. It is obvious that he admires Mr. Gatt very much. I do not know if these are Mr. Gatt's words or not.

Then I posed another question: Suppose someone, the government, said the bells were making too much noise and you could not ring the bells in the evening, say the Tal-Imwiet, after a certain hour- would this upset many people? I received a very positive and immediate response on this one, "Yes." I gathered some people would be up in arms. Here (bait, bait) Joe mentioned the Pater Noster. I played dumb, and got the whole tale again. Because many Inglesi are not like you, they do not like the bells and the Archbishop wrote to the parishes, and the priests told the sextons not to ring the Pater Noster before 6 AM. Many people thought this was a serous thing, and felt very strongly about it, and very much missed the Pater Noster at 4 - even after 3-4 years now? The sexton added that Zejtun did not ring it, and also omitted the Ta L-orazjona.

The session ended abruptly, as it was almost time for the Sexton to ring the Tal- Imiet back at the church. Driving back Joe and Mr. Grec talked a lot in Maltese. Joe told me the Sexton was a simple man and enjoyed riding in a car and being taken to people's homes.

I left Joe and Mr. Grec off at the square, along with the Sexton (who quickly disappeared into the church). By that time I had made up my mind that I had had enough of Joe, who was not a good informant. Joe tried to set another time, but I thanked him profusely and said I had enough information.

Driving back to Hal-Tmiem, I stopped the car to listen for the Tal-Imwiet. It rang 13 times, loud and clear. Joe had said 12 times for this bell. This is the second occasion I have heard it ring 13 times; what gives? Get someone else and get back to that sexton!

Back up for another tale of Lucy's Bar, that occurred on the night of Friday, July 14th, after I finished my notes for the morning and afternoon. Moral: don't be so smug about keeping your field notes up. No day is ever "finished." Norma and Marcia had made an appointment to copy a tape at Lucy's Bar. We loaded the equipment and left bout 8:15, having waited a respectable time to see if Johnny would show up.

The bar was deserted except for the family, an occasional stranger or so who wandered in and out, and Salvu Ragel in his tan Panama hat sitting at the right corner table next to the bar with his feet dangling. He is a very small man, but this evening he was very friendly, and bought a round of drinks for us. I had an early impression of Ragel as a silent, cunning, evil old man from the first time I heard him sing at the Rediffusion. He looked so evil and demonic as he sung, but that is evidently caused by the facial contortion necessary to the singing style. Mose was there, and Carmen and the Attractive P., besides Lucy and a chubby but pleasant girl with short black hair. Mose talked to me about the deficiencies of the upright Akai tape deck on the counter: one of the channels was weak. I inspected the tape heads. He said that the recorder heads had been replaced by a repairman, and I suspected that the rec/playback head had not been aligned properly. Marcia and Norma wanted to dub a tape of Scheychel's that Lucy had borrowed. We had too much difficulty with the connections and the signal to noise ratio. We had brought both Nagra tape decks. Actually, we were going to dub Norma and Marcia's tape of last Saturday for Lucy first. We gave it up and made a dub for Lucy on the two Nagras. Norma gave her a reel of tape. Then we tried to do the other tape, but there was too much noise on it. Carmen brought in an older Phillips tape recorder and we managed to hook it into one of the Nagras. We could not dub on the Nagras because the tape was stereo $1/4^{th}$ track and had something else on the back. It was a poor recording, with flutter hiss and dropout and we later found we would not have enough tape for both sides, because the original was 1- mil tape and we had left only a single reel of 1.5 mil tape. The Nagras are full track. The dub came off poorly. I doubt it will be of much use.

Business began to pick up about 10:30, and a row of men began to fill up the four tables opposite where we were recording. Marcia had a funny encounter with Lucy, trying to buy Ragel a Kinnie. Lucy said they were out of Kinnies, but Marcia saw she had a dozen or so bottles left. There was a price war on soft drinks going on and maybe Lucy was trying to save the Kinnies for her regular customers. When Marcia explained who she wanted the drink for, it was deposited on the counter without further ado. Ragel was in and out of the bar several times, but finally left before it got crowded. He shook our hands all around.

While waiting for the copies to run off, I undertook to repair some banna plugs- nasty things. I had almost finished when I dropped the tiny screw from the barrel off onto the floor. When we began searching for it, a host of people came over and started scraping the floor. Mose appeared with a broom and swept until the screw finally appeared. He said "What's the matter with you, you drunk?"(Kidding) On my second try, the damn screw fell to the floor again, but I found it. The third try was a repeat of the first, broom and all. I finally got it fixed, but I asked Mose to stand by with the broom, just in case. They will talk about it for weeks. During all this, I noticed the Attractive P. kept herself apart from the rest, playing noisily with the small child in one corner. Mose, who was trying to listen to a tape, told her not to make so much noise. We were also trying to listen to the quality bud check of a tape. She continued to play with the child. It seemed almost as if she was deliberately calling attention to herself and trying to cause and argument. When the customers began coming in, she disappeared into the back with the rest of the women, save Lucy and Carmen.

Before we left, Norma bought a round for the house. I don't think I have ever paid for anything I consumed in Lucy's bar. (Next time, I will try to buy a round.)

Questions:

1. Is there a "new" system?
   Besides the Pater Noster change?
   When did it start?
   What churches use it?
   Why did it come about, what reasons for change?
2. Is there an older, traditional system?
   Was it used by all churches, a kind of standard?
   What did it consist of?
   What churches, besides Marsaxlokxx use it?
3. If no definite distinction, what compromises have been made?
4. Have some ringers given up in disgust? Viz: Zejtun.
5. I gather no further edicts have been forthcoming from the Archbishop, but have the progressive priests insisted on altering the bell patterns- shortening them, perhaps?

Sunday, July 16

Kirkop, Ghaxaq, the wedding reception.

I got up late, breakfast of corn flakes and strawberries. Work on field notes. Johnny S. and his brother, Carmen (the only unmarried brother) drove up in Carmen's white Anglica (the one we had followed to Zabbar on the night of June 3rd). Johnny had come to see if Norma was coming "to sea" with them. Marcia went in and told Norma they were here. In a few minutes she appeared. Johnny explained carefully that if she was to go, she could come to their farm outside Marsaskala, the one we had driven to July 2, at quarter to 1. Norma agreed to leave at 12:30. Marcia would drive her over, and then return. Neither Marcia nor I had any eyes for the beach.

After Marcia returned I asked her advice on hitting another village, a small one, either Marsaskala or Kirkop. She said Kirkop would be better, as I might have a chance to confirm, expand or correct what Boissevian had to say about the bells there. She seemed to think I would find the parish priest out and about as it was his workday, so I took off, after eating a Spam sandwich for lunch. Evidently the shortest distance on the map is not always the best route. Marcia advised me to take the long way, around Luqa, rather than direct through Ghaxaq and Gudja, as the roads were narrow and treacherous through these towns.

I soon came upon Kirkop, after rounding the run about near the airport and one other. Although the road I was on seemed to be entering the town at an angle to the church, it soon twisted on it. I went a little way further down the road, hoping to find an inconspicuous parking place, but gave it up when the road went crazy, it got more and more narrow and threatened to take me out of the town. I turned around and drove back to the Pjizza and parked the car opposite the busses. There is no use in trying to act nonchalant, or to try to be un-noticeable, especially if you have a full beard, American clothes, fairly long hair, and metal framed glasses and are 6'1" tall. Brother, are you noticed!

I looked behind the church for the parish priest's house and then wandered down the road in front of the church for a space, but I didn't find the familiar sign with a coat of arms. Going back to the church, I paused and took what I hope is a good –angled shot of the front of the church, a little to the left of the picture in Hal-Farrug. Returning to the square, I saw a man in a clerical black shirt and white collar about to get into a car. I went up and asked if he could direct me to the parish priest. He said he was the parish priest.

I explained that I wanted some information about the bells, and was it possible to talk to him or someone he could suggest at some convenient time? He said yes, but why not now, if I liked? Please to wait until he took the car to the garage. So I stood around by the bus benches until he drove the car across the street and into a garage.

When I first arrived, there were several busses in the square and a group of 6-7 girls in shorts and miniskirts sitting on the benches. I thought they were quite sexy, and thought what a contrast they made with the sanctity of the old church. They preceded me up the street in front of the church, when I walked that way.

When the priest came back, he said just a minute, and went into the doorway of another garage to speak with someone. When he returned several small boys came with him. We stood for a while in front of the church, as he told me about the bells, naming them for me. Several more small boys appeared out of nowhere. The whole troop followed us up the stairs and out upon the roof. I believe there were five or six. This priest seemed to be a kind of father figure to the boys. I should imagine that given the right age and personality, many priests are looked up to by the young boys. Again, the priest didn't introduce himself. He was of medium height, a little heavy set, with thinning black hair and a fairly dark complexion. He wore trousers and a belt. He seemed very proud of his church and quite knowledgeable about many things, Boissevian's study included.

There were two staircases to the roof. We went through the church (the priest and the boys dipped at the altar on the way by), and took the staircase to the left. Besides the usual dome on the roof, there were two smaller windowless domes to either side. The passage was quite narrow. Fortunately, there was a high wall all around the roof.

Foto 11 Kirkop Boys

Foto12. Kirkop Church

(ex. 13)

Plan of the Kirkop Church:

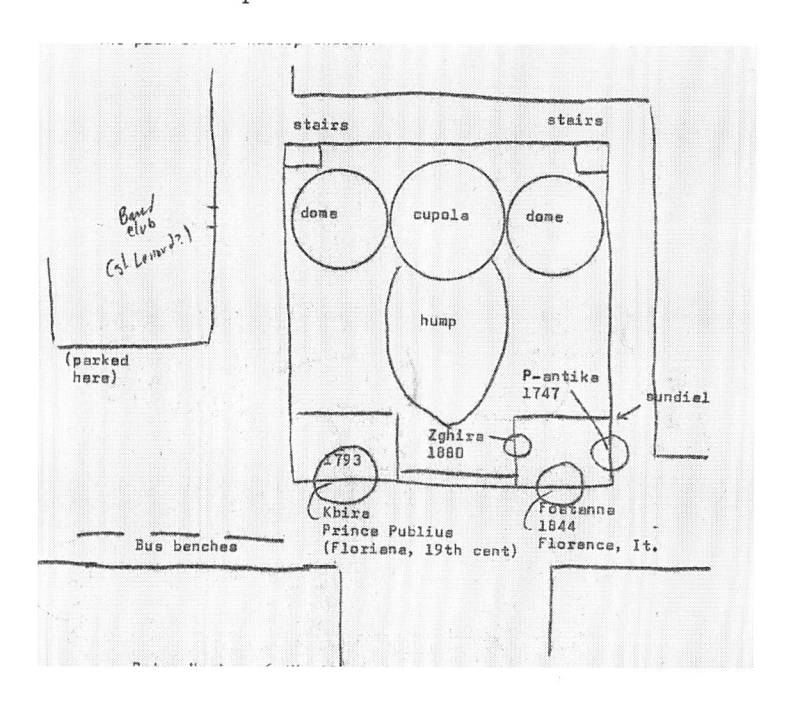

[Plan showing: stairs (top left and right), dome, cupola, dome, hump, Band club (Cal Leonard?), (parked here), P-antika 1747, sundial, Zghira 1880, 1793, Kbira, Foetenna 1844 Florence, It., Prince Publius (Floriana, 19th cent), Bus benches]

Ringings;
Pater Noster: 6 AM, 12 strokes on Kbira Maltese
8 AM, 12 strokes on Kbira   It-Tmienja (8th)
Noon, 12 strokes on Kbira   Nofs inhar (mid-day)
Sunset, 12 strokes on Kbira   Inzul ixxemx

Tal Orazzioni = 1 hour before Tal Imwiet, 1 hour after sunset
Tal Imwiet = 1 hour after Orazzioni, 2 hours after sunset
Sunset (Ave Maria), Orazzioni, Tal Imwiet locked together.
Time is reduced by subtracting, adding 15' per month.
Bells for death and birth: melodies. For birth, Te Deum, or Laude.
Difference recognizable by tempo, character.
Death bells before 8 AM, noon, sunset.

On the roof I took pictures of the bells and got the dates. As usual, the priest said they used the same system as the rest of Malta. He said the bells were very important formerly, when everyone worked in Kirkop, in the village or in the fields. The Pater Noster woke them up, another bell got them to mass, the noon bells told them to eat, the sunset bell told them to stop work, the Orazzjoni to eat, and the Tal Imwiet told them to go to bed.

Nowadays, he said, people only eat and sleep in the villages, commuting to work outside. He also said the times of the masses were arranged by the priests in the village according to the season and the functional needs of going to work. He took me around the edge of the roof and pointed out all the churches you could see; almost all of them were visible. How very small the island, and how very large it seems because of the walls and narrow roads. Actually, all the churches are in sight of one another. Marsaxloxx and Marsaskala on the coast were not visible, because of the scarp.

The priest knew of the bells in B'buga, had wanted to go to the installation there. He said he would try to locate some information he had in his office and mail it to me. I left him my address. He knew where Hal-Tmiem was, because he and some of the boys had gone on a bicycle trip there. He asked me to send him some pictures and any publications in which I might speak about Kirkop. He also suggested I got to Ghaxaq, where he remembered seeing a poster where the rules for the bells were posted.

Earlier, he had pointed out that the roads were completely unplanned. There was some bomb damage during the last war, but the people just rebuilt, without further planning. He showed me that the right windowless dome or bubble (painted red) had been damaged and repaired during the war. It seemed to be covered by a fabric and painted over. On the way down we used the right hand stairs, which were very narrow, steep and wound around a central pole to which I clung. We were soon enveloped in darkness after coming in out of the sun. The electric switch didn't work. After we passed a window further down, I noticed two plaster statues and some flag poles stored in a nitch.

The parish priest was very interested in my work and was very pleasant to me. I thanked him and promised he would hear from me.

I went back to my car and scribbled a few notes and then drove back to the runabout at Luqa airport, and from thence to the entrance to Ghaxaq, which was very narrow indeed. It passes a small church on a hill that is visible from the dual-lane highway. The Ghaxaq church was facing south. After a few turn-arounds I came up behind the church and parked. I got out and made a preliminary stroll around the side of the church and down the long narrow pjazza in front. There were a few bars open, and a goodly number of young and old lounging on the steps of the church, the doorways and the bars.

There were two clubs, St. Joseph and St. Mary, and a garish MLP bar down the street to the left that had a large sign over the door with the names of Libya, America, and several other countries. I walked back up the street in front of the church after taking a picture of the front of the church. I wanted to take a picture of the MLP bar, but there were several young men with long hair lounging outside and I didn't want to antagonize them. I was looking again for the parish priest's house, but again I had no luck. I took another slide of a building in back of the church; the upper story of which was decorated gingerbread style to the glory of Mary of the Assumption, the titular saint. St. Joseph is evidently the secondary saint.

Since I hadn't located the priest, I went in the right transept door. As usual, there was a man there, white shirt, black trousers, sitting and staring fixedly at the altar. But he looked up and said hello. I assumed it was not out of the question to speak to him, so I asked where I could find the parish priest. He said the priest was not here now, but I could go around the corner inside the church and see the statue of Mary (a Mary pusher, evidently). I explained I was here to see the bells. I got the standard abbreviated explanation of how they ring the bells every quarter hour during the festal etc. so I thanked him and slipped inside to see the statue (I said).

Actually, I never located the statue. My attention was drawn to a very old woman seated far back in the right hand side of the church in what appeared to be a carrying chair. As I drew closer, I recognized the large black hood held in an arch by some frame. She was wearing the traditional purdah-like costume for matrons. I did my glide around the interior of the church. The large front doors were closed- when are they opened? and covered with drapes. I stole several glances at the old woman, who was staring at the altar without expression. She was extremely thin and fragile.

I went back outside by a door a little further from the transept door. Since the group at the MLP had disappeared, I walked down and snapped a picture of the front. I always have trouble focusing the camera because of my glasses, so it took me longer than I might have wished. Several youths were glaring at me from the tables inside. Why do I assume the MLP lads are antagonistic to strangers? Am I intimidated by young men with long hair, who seem loud and voluble? Do I know they are talking about me? Is it necessarily in derogative terms, i.e. "look at the fool Inglese tourist out there"- so what?

This time I went up the street and into the St. Joseph Band Club and got a Coke. There was a pool game in the large room in back. The pool table was very large. I noticed a sign in Maltese and English, "no smoking please." I stood up at the bar, because the small table in front of it was occupied, and the only other table was ostentatiously placed in front of the pool table and was completely unoccupied. There were a large number of young men lined up directly in back of the pool table, watching the game.

After about 4 minutes, a chubby blind boy was led up to the bar. The young man behind the bar, a slender fellow, pale, with short hair and sideburns, about 25, brought out a coke and placed his hands on the bottle and the glass. They conversed for a while. Then the Blind Boy turned in my general direction and began a conversation in excellent English. He excused himself, said I had been seen taking pictures, and wondered what my interest was. Hagg! I thought, they sent for the local witch!

I explained my interest in the bells. I don't remember the exact order of the conversation. We talked for about 20 or 30 minutes. First he talked about himself, about his blindness and what he was trying to accomplish. He was going to school and taking an advanced degree (not the university). I told him about Karen Nielsen, the blind girl at ECU who was so exceptionally well trained and whom I admired very much. He said he had to read braille, he could touch type on the typewriter (I said I could only hunt and peck) and that all his books in braille come from England, as it would not be economical to do Maltese books in braille. His watch was a braille watch. He said he had an Alsatian dog, but that it was not professionally trained. He got around mostly with the white cane.

The boy's eyes seemed normal, except they rolled about without looking anywhere. When we began to talk about the bells in Ghaxaq, he said everything could be arranged for me very easily, since everyone was very proud of the bells and the church and would be eager to help. He said there were 6 bells. He began to ask the bar tender about some of the names. The youth behind the bar spoke almost no English, or he wasn't willing to speak much. He became more interested and friendly as we talked, and offered me a cigarette, which I finally accepted and which he lit. I had forgotten to bring my pipe, damn it.

Two of the bells: Kbira, "Marjii," and Don Marcell. The others he was not sure of. The Blind Boy (and he introduced himself and I didn't get his name… shame!) said that in olden times they used to ring the bells whenever a severe storm frightened them. He said they no longer do it in Malta, but they still do it in Gozo. His implication was that it was an act of superstitious terror, no longer necessary in modern Malta and that Gozo, being a little backward, still did it. The subject turned to Easter. The bells are stopped on Good Friday and re-began in a massed peal at the 8 PM mass on Sunday.

I asked about the wooden thing they used instead of the bells. He told me its name was "cuqlajta. It is the Maltese word for "rattle. Maltese always seems to have a lot of silent syllables. He seemed to pronounce it "cho-li-tah". The bartender drew me a picture of it on a piece of cardboard. He explained (through the other) that there were 14 spokes, and that each were struck by two wooden hammers when the affair was rotated. I had been assuming up until this time that the device was some kind of huge wooden ratchet. They said it was kept on the steeple and that once a man was almost knocked off the roof while running it. When I asked again about when the bells where stopped and stared during Easter. Actually, I suggested the bells were stopped on Maundy Thursday, darn it, I must not falsify these notes. Anyway, they said the bells stopped on Maundy Thursday- I was right- and restarted where? The Gloria? Ah, you know the Gloria? Yes it was the Gloria.

I led the conversation around to what people thought about the bells. The Blind Boy said yes, there had been a large controversy about it in the newspaper.

Also, he mentioned there had been a nasty competition between the two band clubs some years ago.

Then he consulted his watch and said we could go to see the bells if I liked, he would show them to me. He went into consultation with the lad behind the bar, and a small boy with freckles and long brown hair was summonsed. The younger boy was about 10, with large blue eyes. Later, the Blind Boy explained that the younger boys loved to lead him around, and he imagined this one was in 7th heaven by now.

As we left the Band Club, I thanked the bartender and shook his hand. I caught him a little awkwardly as he was lifting one section of the bar to come out and he dropped it on himself. The younger boy and BB went out of the bar with me following. They made a strange pair, the BB holding onto the boy's left arm. The young boy hardly came up to his shoulder.

Foto 13: Ghaxaq: B.B. and his young boy guide in bell tower:

Actually, the BB did very well and was evidently used to getting around. He seemed to know exactly where he was headed, and only the small details had to be filled in for him. I can't imagine how I would do under the same circumstances. We went to the left transept entrance. At the door we could hear a service in progress. The reason we had waited in the bar, I remember now, was that the parish priest had not yet returned from his home, which was some distance off. Now it was 4 PM and the priest was back, but the service was not yet over.

The BB insisted that we cross the transept and go into the vestry, even though the service was still going on. I felt very uneasy, but I have always found that people don't mind you creeping about in their churches. Guess I am over reacting to the strangeness and the opulence of the churches. In the back we found a priest at a desk pouring over some notes. He said the parish priest was over there, by the altar, and we checked in back by the choir stalls and confirmed on for a while, and we walked back across the transept and out into the doorway. The door to the bell tower was opened and the young boy and the BB mounted the stairs. BB said to come and close the door. He had remarkable little trouble mounting the long staircase, and would call out warning whenever he brushed against a wire or a piece of rope from the bell.

Just before we came out on the roof, we paused to examine the clock mechanism in the space directly below the stage-right bell tower. It was a large rectangular frame with cogs, suspended weights and a short pendulum. BB said it was always going wrong. I checked to see if there was enough light for a picture, but there wasn't. I noticed some bottles with the remains of candles on a window ledge. Blind boy asked if a candle would help, but I said no.

The clock mechanism: (ex. 14)

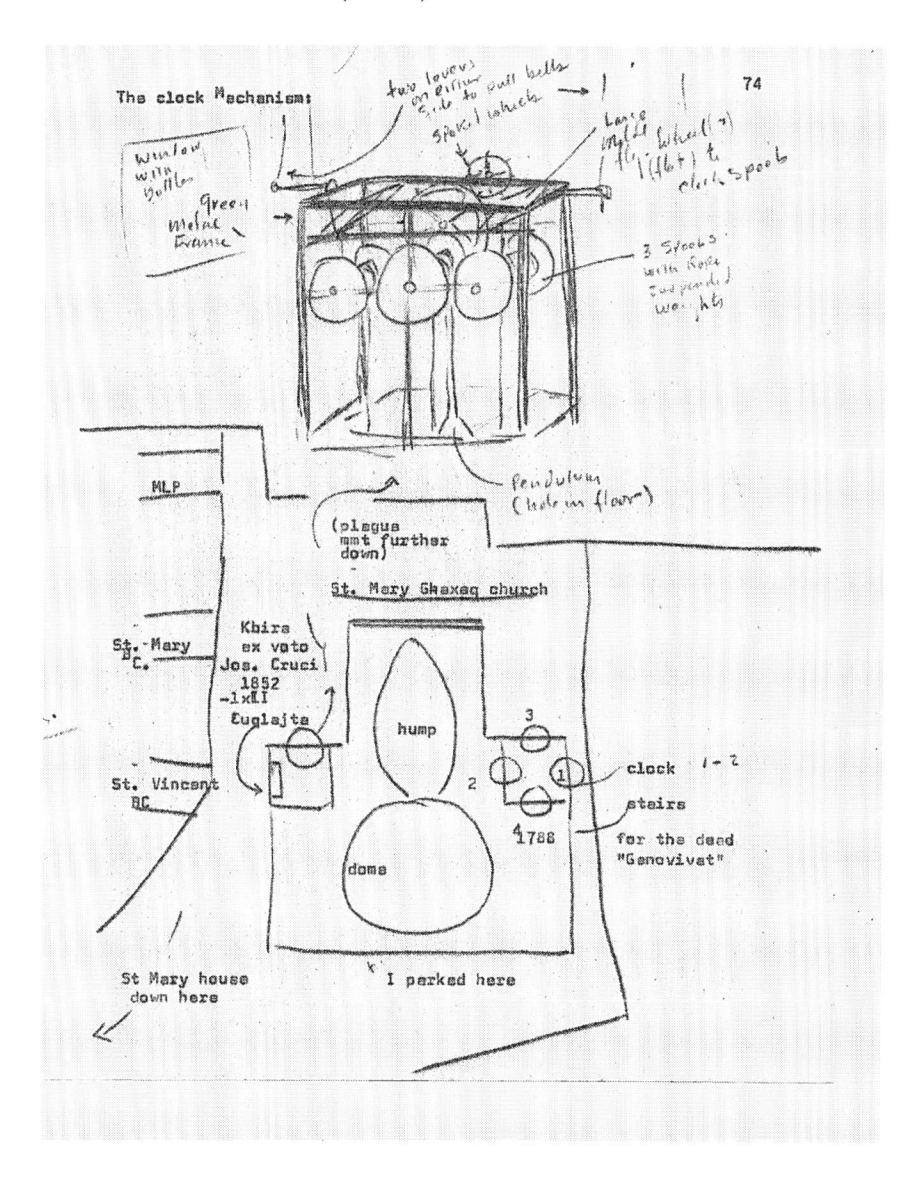

As close as I can remember (I have had a little trouble here in remembering the sequence), we came out on the roof and walked around the dome to the stage-right tower, which contained a large bell "Kbira" and the Cuqlajta rattle. I took a picture of the bell and two of the rattle. As usual, the inscription on the bell was difficult to read. I saw the date MDCCCLXII- 1864, right? A small marble plaque to the right read "Ex voto Joseph Cruci, 1852." The bell had a Maltese cross and I could see the inscription "Klerl."

The Cuqlajta looked like a wheel about three feet in diameter with the rim removed and the spokes replaced with wooden hammers hinged to the axle.

ex. 15: cuqlajta

[Sketch: Crudely; Two wooden hammers fixed b/tw ea. spoke. [there were many more "spokes" than this]. There was a handle on the axle to turn it with.]

Then we went across the roof hump to the stage right bell tower. This tower contained four bells. The two bells mounted on the side were controlled by the clock. The bell in back was dated 1788. Blind Boy said it was used for the dead. I saw the inscription "Genovivat" on its side. The smallest bell, which I think was attached to the clock and which hung to the far right, was called "Maria."

These names and positions are tentative as my sketches are confusing and I will have to recheck them.

We then went back downstairs. Blind Boy had kept up a running conversation, but I was too busy with the camera and the sketches to contribute much. The young boy asked if the bells were going to be on the TV. I suppose be spoke little or no English, because Bind Boy spoke quite freely in front of him.

Downstairs, we again traipsed across the transept. The service was still going on. The other priest said the parish priest was perhaps finished by now, so we went again behind the altar. This time I succeeded in introducing myself to the parish priest, who actually told me his name (and I forgot it again). I asked my main question, about the list of bell ringings the priest in Kirkop had mentioned. I was taken back into the vestry and shown an oblong typed and enumerated list about 2" long and enclosed in a glass case. It was in Maltese. Blind Boy said he would be very glad to translate it for me. I suggested that I bring my tape recorder Tuesday at 10:30. Blind Boy said he would meet me in the band club and bring a friend to read the Maltese.

We stayed for a while, talking to the parish priest, who was very pleasant and attentive. I learned the parish priest from Kirkop was actually from Ghaxaq. The old sexton in Zejtun can sing and recognize practically every bell in Malta. The old sexton in Ghaxaq has retired. The sweetest bells in Malta are those of St. Dominic in Valletta, they are similar or equal to the bells of St. Peters in the Vatican in Rome. Guliano Eauci made the big bell at B'Kara & made most big bells in Malta. While he knew how to make the bells wells, he didn't tune them well, so that the bells in Malta are perhaps not so well tuned as elsewhere. There is a bell to announce birth. The new father comes to the church when the mother goes into labor and the bell is rung. Bells are repaired in the dockyards. 30-40 years ago, a bell fell out of the tower at Ghaxaq and had to be repaired there.

The young boy had left by this time, so I led Blind Boy out and took him back to the band club. On the way he spoke to several people in the doorways. He said everyone knew him and that it was easy therefore for him to arrange things for me (watch out not to get "owned."). I left him at the door of the Band Club, where a man took him over at the entrance. He said he did not have his cane today, and needed assistance to the door.

I said goodbye, and went back to my car behind the church. Someone had parked a Morris Minor in front of it and I could not get out. I knew all I had to do was walk up and scratch my head. Immediately, a couple of matrons sitting on some steps began gesturing up an ally and a small boy was sent running off to fetch the owner, who soon appeared and backed up for me.

Really, this culture is a piece of cake. I could fall on my face and be picked up several times a day and get dusted off and fed into the bargain.

From the Blind Boy: Old people still miss the bell (Pater Noster) to wake up by, and get ready for mass. The younger people now work in factories. They work in shifts and have to sleep late. Joe Attard worked sometimes in the morning, sometimes evening. Rather, he told me he worked the early and the late shift. I gather he ran a crane at an incinerator. We had to schedule our sessions with Mr. Gatt around his shifts.

Monday July 17

Marcia left early for shopping in Valletta (about 7am) and returned about 10 with huge gobs of food- a real go-getter. She had only been able to get a one case of lemonade from Tony's (Marsaxlokk) because he was not buying soft drinks and beer due to the increase of prices at the factory on one hand, and the limitation of prices by the government on the other. Seems like there is always a problem like this with someone caught in the middle- like the parish priest, or Tony.

Did I mention somewhere that you couldn't drink the tap water because Malta was largely limestone? It had other undesirable things in it as well.

So, I loaded some empty bottles in the boot of the car in hopes I could locate some drinks on the way back from Mdina, at the Farsons plant. I went through Hamrun again and was held up by the traffic. It seemed backed up going out of Marsa, for some reason I could not see. There were many more military vehicles on the road; most of them supply services trucks.

I got to Mdina at the stroke of 11. I paused to take the last two frames in my camera, of the cathedral and of a smaller church down the street. Several men were putting up poles in preparation for the festal.

In the museum, the attendant went to get Father Azzopardi. I took the opportunity to change the film in my camera. Father Azzopardi, who always has definite ideas about what I should see, in what order, took me first to see an old upright organ that used to be carried in processions. He called one of the caretaker-restorers whom I had seen there before, a pleasant, handsome man of about 40 with shirt and narrow tie and dark complexion. He talked at length about the organ and disassembled the front so we could see the tracker action. He said his father worked on this organ, and that his grandfather had also worked at the museum, in the job he now occupied. He said many churches did not have organs, and that this organ was probably taken wherever there was a festival in the old days.

The organ:

(ex. 16)

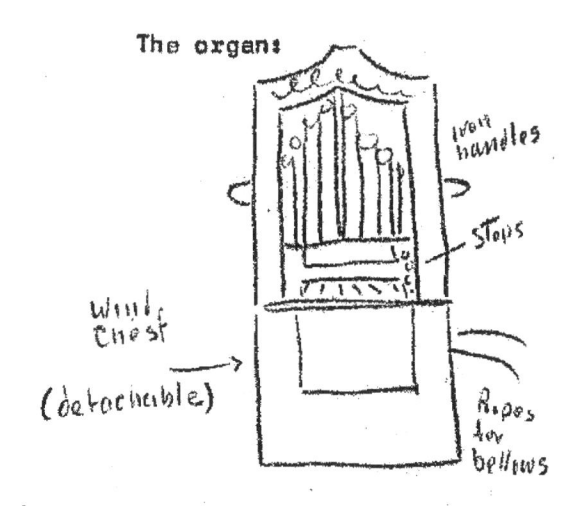

Beside the organ hung a wooden cover that had been removed from the organ in the cathedral. It was decorated with a somewhat crude picture of St. Cecilia, and bore the name "Dominicus Autorus Rossi, Neapolitanus, Regiae Cappellae Suae Maiestatis, Organaris Fecit AD 1774."

Having exhausted this topic, Father Azzopardi led me out the door and across the street to the left door of the Cathedral. He rang a small bell to be admitted, and sent me to admire the interior while he fetched a key. He wanted me to see the other organ, before we went up on the roof. The interior was deserted. Talk about opulence! The shrine to the right of the altar was decorated for some ceremony. Looked like Christmas in there, in silver and gold, literally. Father Azzopardi found me after a bit and led the way out the door, pausing to show me the carving. We went up a flight of stairs and into the narrow organ loft where there was a decrepit one manual organ with a narrow keyboard and tiny set of pedals. He asked me to play it for the sound. Evidently it is not used. There was an electric switch, but pushing it produced no effect. Father Azzopardi went in back and threw a switch and the blower went on. I could hear the air hissing, and then he uttered an exclamation ("OOO, something is happening") and asked me to come in back of the organ. The large fabric billows were pushing up a wooden platform about the size of a door on which some limestone weights had been placed. "What is happening," he wanted to know. The platform was rising mysteriously, like some saint being elevated to heaven. I explained and went back and played the organ for a while. The keys were sticky and the pipes needed tuning. Father Azzopardi asked my opinion, and I said I wasn't an organist, but I thought the instrument merited restoration.

Finally, we made our way to the roof and the bell towers. We were late for the 12 o'clock ringing; I saw one of the chaps in cap, loose trousers and vest pulling the ropes from just within the door to the front of the church on the stage right door we had entered. Father Azzopardi took me up a long flight of stairs to a hallway that used to be the Cathedral museum. He said it was too old and musty and didn't attract many tourists, so they had moved across the street into the present quarters. It was used for storage now.

The plan on the roof:

(ex. 17)

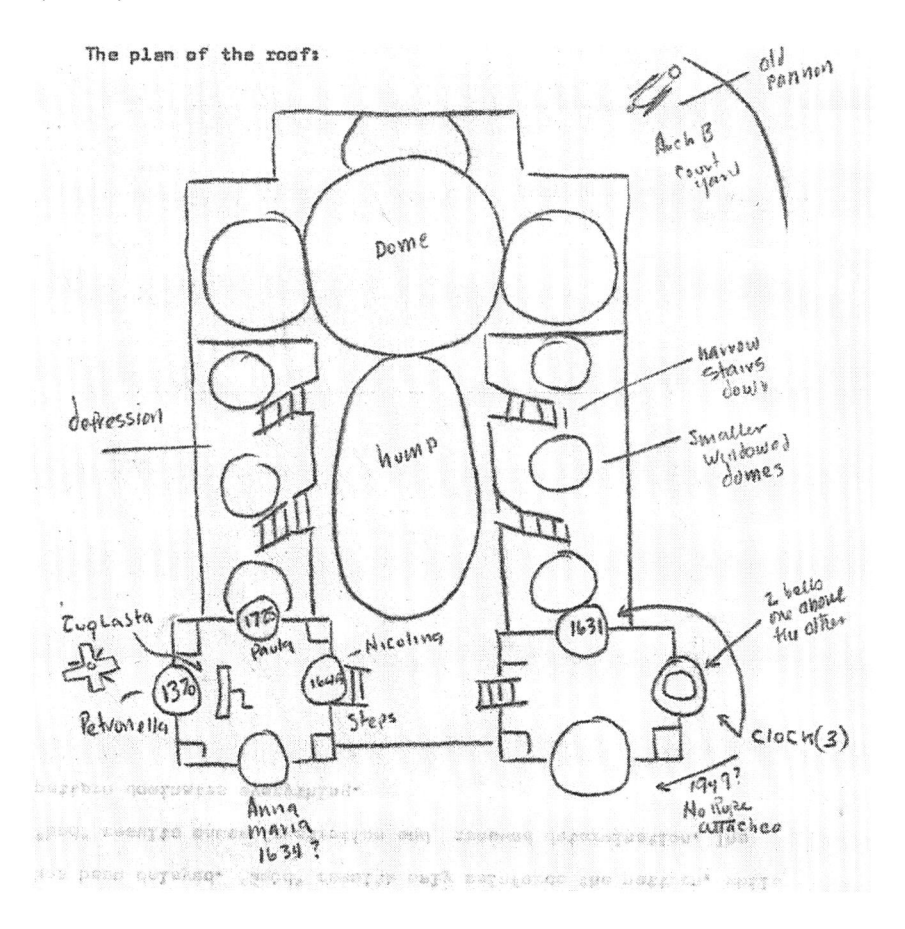

The plan of the roof:

[hand-drawn diagram showing the roof plan with labels: old cannon, Arch B courtyard, Dome, narrow stairs down, smaller windowed domes, depression, hump, 2 bells one about the other, clock(3), 1947? No figure attached, ZugLasta, 1370, Petronella, 1775, Paula, 1648, Nicolina, steps, 1631, Anna Maria 1634?]

Foto14: Fr. Azzopardi on Mdina roof:

We climbed first into the stage-right tower, the left one from the front on the diagram. There were four bells there, plus a dilapidated cuqlajta (the Easter "Rattle"). The bell, called "Petronella," was very old and crusted with stains. It bore the image of a rampart lion and the picture of a saint. It was longer and narrower than other bells I had seen. I took some pictures. Father Azzopardi said the Cuqlajta was still used- they were very conservative there.

Foto15. Mdina roof and ornamental wall supports

Over in the front-right tower, where the clock bells were hung, I explained the striking system to Father Azzopardi who really hadn't figured it out until I explained it. The three bells were tuned high-bell, major-7th, and octave below. The other bell on the front of the tower was not connected by a bell rope to the downstairs. Father Azzopardi said it dated from about 1949. We went into the closet below the bells and examined the clock mechanism, which was similar to that of Ghaxaq but in much better repair. It had 4 weights, a much longer pendulum and was wound every day.

Father Azzopardi paused on the way out to chip away the plaster from an inscription. I believe it was in Italian. It said something to the effect that so-and-so had been hanged in April of 1723 for the murder of his wife, so-and-so.

In one of the towers, Father Azzopardi said they had a man who only rang the bells (a specialist) but that he had retired. I could not get him to say his name, because he changed the subject.

By this time, it was nearing 1 PM and Father's lunch hour. We had a leisurely stroll around the roof. I noticed an old signal cannon deserted in the courtyard over to the right of the church. Father Azzopardi made a note to haul it in and repair it for the museum.

Once downstairs, I began asking some pointed questions and the priest accosted a young man standing in the hall and asked him about the bell ringing. Back over in the museum, another man and the attendant were pressed into service. Father left to get his briefcase, and I was able to question them alone. They were closing the museum, and Father was in a hurry to leave. We shook hands after the door was locked and he got in a small brown car to be taken somewhere.

Foto 16: oldest bell

Summary of what I managed to wheedle out of Father and the others:

The Angelus: one of 4 times during the day that the angel might have appeared to the Virgin Mary (they aren't taking any chances)
Pater Noster, 8 AM, 12 noon and sunset. 9 strokes with Nicolina
Masses: no fixed rules. 10 strokes
Tal-Imwiet: 9 strokes on Nicolina (No. 4). Father said 9 was a biblical number.
Mota Tal Hamis, Friday at 3 PM. Mdina and St. John's do not ring this mota, as they are cathedrals and not mere parish churches. They are above the parish churches, a higher order, and do not have the Via Crucis devotions.
Tal-orazzijoni: unknown
Death bell: Nicolina again.
Funeral Bells: two small bells for ordinary people, 2 large bells for priests and other important people. Some melodies are played for the funerals, lasting 15 minutes.
The ringing to call the churches: Father Azzopardi had mentioned this ringing before, lamenting that they no longer did it. The young attendant in the lobby said this was done with two preliminary peals and then all together: Tin, tin, boom. Tin, tin, boom.
The consecration of new bells: also described by the attendant. The bell is placed in the church yard and decorated. The priest blesses it, christens it, and gives it a name. Sometimes it is carried in a procession. Then it is hung in the belfry.
Ringing during storms: Father Azzopardi said they still do it.
Guliano Cauci, the bell-maker, had a shop at Ghayn Dwieli
Sanctus of the mass: bells rung at signal. The higher the occasion, the more bells are rung.
The Angelus 12 PM: it was stuck while Father Azzopardi and I were going up the stairs. It seems to me that at least two if not three bells were sounded according to some pattern I didn't catch.

After parting from Father Azzopardi (with some relief) I went back to the parking lot and got a sandwich and Coke at the outdoor shop there with the BP flag. I checked the Point De View hotel's restaurant, but it was deserted and I could hear the servers eating in the kitchen.

While I was seated eating and scribbling some notes, a perfectly awful set of Limeys came up, cursing and fussing. There was an older couple, a young red-faced fat blonde of about 25 and two dark young men (Maltese tour guides?) fussing about. The two men and the girl went inside while the older couple remained seated at the table next to me. Bitch, bitch, bloody this and that. They seemed very unpleasant.

After I had relaxed and lit a pipe, I went back to the car, paid the floppy old man who is the watch dog there, took a leak in the john across the street- the one with flowers and cigarette cans all over the place- paid 4₵ to the attendant, and took off for St. Paul's in Rabat, which I eventually found.

I parked the car in a parking lot across from the church and took some pictures of the church and the walkway and statue to the left. I also canvassed the bell towers, taking notes. To the left front of the church, there was a separate entrance. A sign announced it was St. Paul's Grotto. I had noticed a bar called the "Grotto Bar" and another across from it called "St. Paul's Bar" (sic!). I entered and went down a flight of stairs to an iron grill. Immediately the lights began going on and a pale youth of about 20 came down and gave me the standard tourist spiel. St. Paul had been shipwrecked off Gozo and had spent a number of days in Malta, where he converted Publius, the Roman governor. He spent I think, 6 days in a cave to the right, which the guide opened for me. The guide explained that the cave used to be connected to the old Christian catacombs, but the passageways had been sealed up. He then took me into some smaller shrines and indicated a plate where I could leave a donation to the church. I left 30₵ because I intended to pump him.

After he finished his spiel, I gave him mine about the bells. Sure enough, he helped to ring the bells and would be glad to show them to me. He took me upstairs and delivered me into the care of an older man, while he went to get some keys. I got a tour of the paintings and the relics. Finally, the young man reappeared and took me out the left front entrance steps, who should I see but Father Azzopardi flapping past. He called out to me before I could duck in. The young man also greeted him. Father Azzopardi said "Well I see you have got your way" and flapped on. Earlier he had suggested that I come to him at some unspecified date in the future and he would take me to see this church. I learned on the way up that Father Azzopardi was connected to this church in some manner.

Ex. 18 The plan of St. Paul's in Rabat:

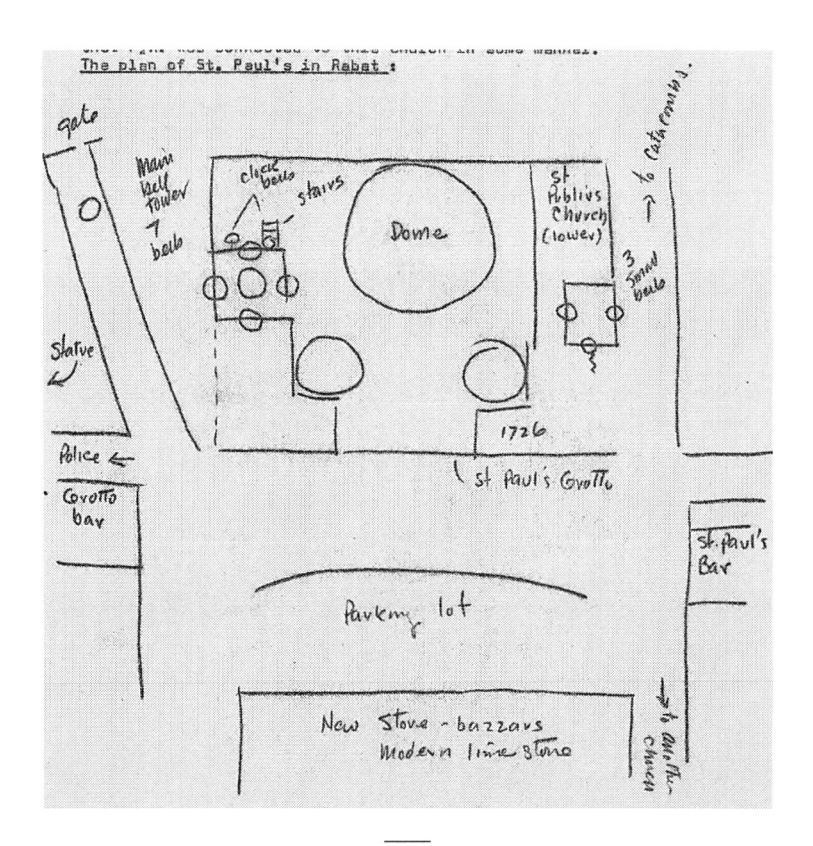

There was only a single bell tower connected to St. Paul's proper. The bells to the right front belonged to St. Publius. There were 7 bells crowded into the tower, all dating from 1911:

(ex. 19)

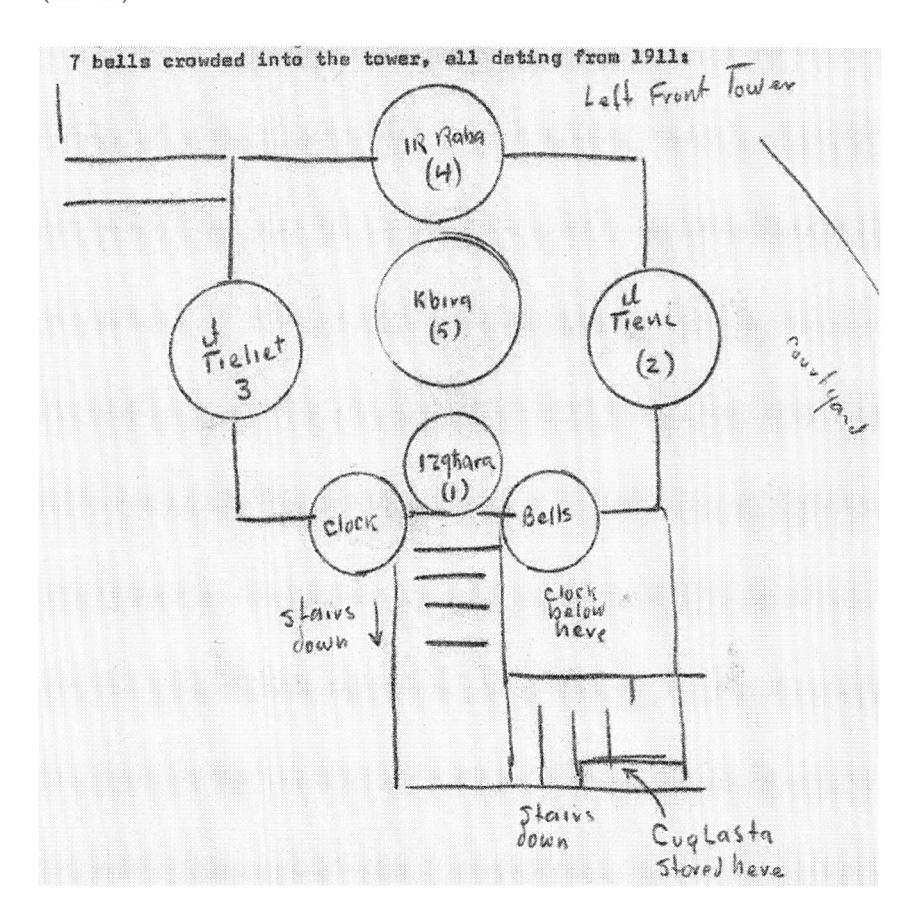

```
7 bells crowded into the tower, all dating from 1911:
                                              Left Front Tower
                    IR Raba
                      (4)

          Kbira           il
           (5)          Tienc
 il                      (2)
Tieliet
   3                                          courtyard
                   Izghara
                     (1)
         Clock              Bells

        Stairs               Clock
        down                 below
                             here

                          Stairs
                          down      Cuqlasta
                                    stored here
```

On the way up we paused to examine the usual clock mechanism in the area below the bells. There was also a wooden cuqlajta stored in the stairwell. The young man talked to me for quite a while. He seemed to know a lot about the motas used for feasts, and gave me several patterns. When I began to bear down on the daily bells, he began to act confused and unsure. He gave me his name and address: Sammut Laurence, 3/A2 St. Kataldris Street, Rabat. I gave him my address at Hal Tmiem and he said he was going to find out for me exactly and write.

Summary of daily bells at St. Pauls:

>Pater Noster: not rung (?)
>Angelus: 8 AM, Sunset, 8 or 9 strokes, Kbira
>Orazzijoni: unknown
>Tal Imwiet: 7 PM Ir Raba (4) How many strokes?
>Funeral procession: Izghara, It Tien (12, 12, 12, etc.) Until return
>Mota Tal Hamis: good, definite description. Like change ringing? Each bell enters slowly and works up to double stroke. The bells then leave off one by one until the first to begin is left alone.

The last bell stops abruptly, the 1 stroke is added as punctuation. For the Thursday mota, the order is 1, 2, 3, 4, 5, (4, 3, 2, 1), from the smallest to the largest and back to the smallest.

>Tal Tlieta (3 PM Friday): a melodic order, 1, 2, 23, 34, 45.
>Intervals: 1-2 = ½ step. 2-3, major 3rd.
>Motas for processions: 5, 4, 3, 2, 1, 2, 3, 4, 5
>Mota for feast day: begin on 4. Assume it is 4, 3, 2, 1, 5 (Fri, Sat)
>The Barca & Te Deum (new terms): all five at once. Someone counts, "1, 2, 3, 4, -boom." Barca is used whenever the sacrament is brought out of the church. The Te Deum is used day before feast in the evening, about sunset (7 PM)
>Tone Syllables for the bells: tin, tan, tone, tawn, boom. (for 1-5)

Foto 17 St. Paul's church

Sammut was very sure about the motas and the bells that require more than one person, but he was unsure about single ringings.

While we were talking in the tower, an older man came up and started talking. He was about 45, slender, grey hair with some black, and dark. I could barely understand his English. He started to ask me some questions, had I been here or there. Summut seemed annoyed. I thought it was the sacristan and tried to understand what it was he was talking about. Sammut seemed to give up in disgust. The older man kept up a steady stream as we went down the stairs. It wasn't until after Sammut said goodbye and promised again to write that I began to realize that the man was some kind of tour guide. Insofar as I had already departed from Sammut, I let him take me up the street to a smaller church where he showed me some relics, St. Paul's knuckle bone, St. Matthew's fingernail etc. Downstairs were some of the catacombs with open graves and the dust and remnants of bones. The man said the place had been used as an air raid shelter during the war.

I left 10¢ in the coin box. He took me up the street where there were some entrances and ventilation holes for the catacombs, then he wanted me to go into a craft shop nearby, but I was thoroughly disgusted with myself for falling for a tour guide leech and said I had to go. The man walked me back to my car and pointed the way out. I got in and drove off. I didn't offer him anything, but he didn't seem disappointed.

Earlier, the guide inside the main church had said that St. Paul's was really older than Mdina: it was the first Christian church on the island. Note: local pride intense.

I drove back past Mdina and took off for Mosta.

Mosta is down in a valley, and the big dome of the sand-red cathedral is visible over everything else. The free-standing dome is said to be the largest in the world. I had often seen it from the roofs of the churches I had visited. Mosta church is completely round, i.e. it consists of a single huge round dome with a façade in front and a lower square building behind.

Foto 18. Mosta church

I parked in front of a souvenir shop and walked to the nearest open bar. It was about 3:30 by then, a time when most shops are closed, except, I supposed, those who remain open to cater to tourists. I was quite tired and wanted some place to sit down and scribble. I went into "Johnny's" bar, across from the church, and got a coke and a candy bar. Sure enough, there were two Inglesi couples at the bar, I took my Coke into a back room and relaxed a bit. I noticed that the 3:30 bell sounded a triad, like this: 5, 3,... 1, 1, 1. The 3:45 bells rang 5, 3, 5, ... 1, 1, 1.

Plan of Mosta Church (St. Mary's) and environs:

(ex. 20)

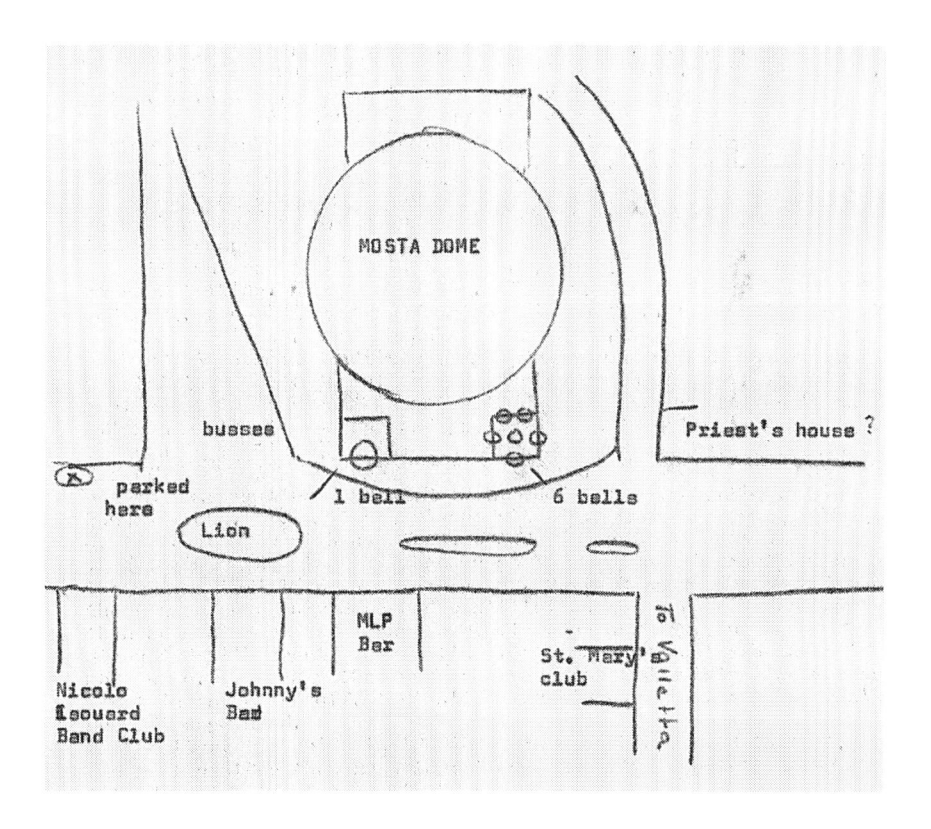

After I finished my coke and candy bar and smoked a pipe, I felt I had my noodle together again, so I ambled out of the bar and walked around the church, drawing a diagram of the square and counting the bells. I went inside the church. I want to call it a cathedral because it seemed so huge and opulent. There were no fixed pews, but a large number of single chairs. The altar was free standing. There was a wooden pulpit, a large wooden column with steps up to a covered place to stand and lecture. These are to be found in almost every church. I presume someone stands up there and orates. This particular one was also free standing. In older churches, it is usually fixed to a column. There were no columns in the Mosta church, and the vast space enclosed by the dome is breathtaking.

There was no priest in sight. I passed one on the way out, but he was already clicking his beads and seemed preoccupied, so I didn't bother him. I strolled down the street to Valletta for a way, pausing to look at some of the stores. Then I got my gumption up and stomped into the MLP bar, which was strategically located almost directly in front of the church, a door or so down from Johnny's bar. The bar itself was located upstairs. I got a Coke from the small counter in the back and sat off to one side. The room contained a number of tables and chairs, some of which were occupied by men and young men of various sizes and descriptions. The older men seemed like middle class laborers. On the walls I saw (besides the picture of Mintoff, the PM), a picture of Pope John XX, right in front, and a religious picture of the Sacred Heart of Jesus. There were some blownup pictures of a mass rally held on the anniversary of the founding of the MLP, date 1956? I recognized the Mosta Church in it.

Most interesting was a single animal horn hanging on the wall with the tip pointed down and a curved lobster claw protruding out the top. It puzzled me for a while, until I recalled that the sign for the MLP is a conical torch with a curved flame. What an ingenious adaptation of a party symbol! The horn is protection against L-graja il Hazina, the evil eye.

No one seemed to pay me the slightest bit of attention. I was nervous and spilled some tobacco from my can on my lap. I decided not to tackle anyone in that state of mind. I don't know, but I guess I think the MLP is a den of animosity and aggression, and I don't want any of it directed towards myself.

I finished my coke and went back outside and walked across the street towards the busses at the curbside. A priest had just walked out of the church It may have been the one I had seen entering the church. I caught up with him, and said "Father, can you help me?" I guess it was either the right or the wrong thing to say, or else there was a note of desperation in my voice. Anyway, he turned around immediately with a benign expression on his face and said "of course, my son, of course." I didn't notice any sign of disappointment on his face as I explained I wanted to study the bells there. He said I should just go inside the church and find the sacristan who was sure to be by the door, and he would take me right up to the towers. He took my arm and led me halfway to the entrance and patted my arm.

However, there was no one remotely resembling a sacristan inside the entrance. I went back outside and read the wedding bans, the prohibition against women entering the church with low necklines, sleeveless blouses or miniskirts. Almost everywhere there is likely to be a poster in English and Maltese calling the attention of the public to a regulation that prohibits indecent exposure etc. This notice is always found outside police stations and it also contains appraisals of the morality of current movies. Most of the notices were disapproving.

At length I noticed an older couple in tourist style clothing examining the altar. A young Maltese man of about 22 accompanied them, and was gesturing and pointing out objects of interest. He was rather short and wore a dark knitted shirt with open collar. His hair was black and a little fuzzy without being overly long. He was obviously a tour guide. He motioned to me and I went over reluctantly. I told him I was interested in the bells, and he said sure, come on with him and he would show them to me in a while. So I accompanied the older couple and got a tour of the vestry and an explanation of the various statues and paintings. In the back was the famous Axis bomb that had come through the dome and skidded across the floor without exploding or hurting anyone.

The older couple was Irish, I think. We exchanged a few comments and pleasantries. After the guide's spiel was ended, the man handed the guide 20¢ and thanked him. Then the young man took me to the front-right or stage left tower, which we climbed. As it was my third steeple of the day, I was somewhat winded by the time we reached the top.

The bell tower contained 6 bells. The guide was unable to name any of them except for the smallest bell, called Angeli, which he said they rung on the death of a small child, because he might become an angel. As usual, the inscriptions on the bells were too high up to read clearly. I did identify two Cauci bells and the date 1825 on the bell in the center. He knew a few occasions on which the bells were rung, and he mentioned that the Pater Noster used to be rung at 3:30 with 33 strokes on the big bell in the other tower. He said that today, people had to work in shifts and that many had to sleep late.

I completed my sketch and we went out on the roof, where I took some pictures. The guide took me up a flight of stairs to a door to the very top of the dome and we looked down into the church. It is strange that I am not experiencing any acrophobia- not that it was ever that serious, but I have always been uneasy about heights since my childhood. There was a capstan mechanism near the door, which the guide said was used to lower and raise some chandeliers for the feasts.

The door to the stage-right tower was locked, so we retraced our steps back to the stage-left tower and went down. The guide said he would take me to the sacristan. On the way down we met another elderly tourist couple making their way up the stairs. I told them to be careful as there were no railings, and one man replied, yes there never were in these places.

Downstairs again, the guide took me back behind the altar into the vestry and into a small room where I found a slender middleaged man counting change from a collection basket. He spoke no English and the guide undertook to get the names of the bells from him. It was a difficult process, with many repetitions. It always is, somehow.

The bells in the stage-right/ front left tower in Mosta:

(ex. 21)

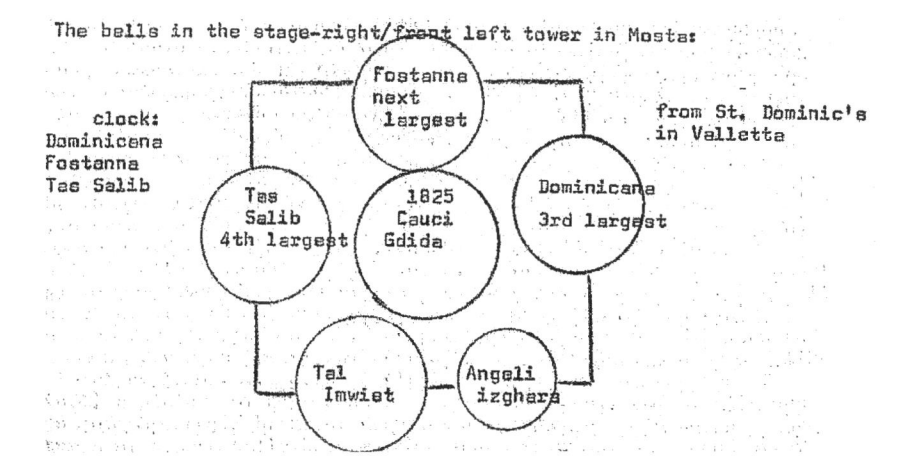

```
The bells in the stage-right/front left tower in Mosta:
                         ┌─────Fostanna─────┐
                         │     next         │
     clock:              │    largest       │          from St. Dominic's
    Dominicana           │                  │           in Valletta
    Fostanna             │                  │
    Tas Salib      ┌── Tas ──┬── 1825 ──┬── Dominicana ──┐
                   │  Salib  │  Cauci   │   3rd largest  │
                   │ 4th largest│ Gdida │                │
                   │         │          │                │
                   └─────────┴── Tal ──┬── Angeli ──────┘
                              Imwiet   │  izghar
```

Summary of bell ringings:

Pater Noster: not rung (except day of feast of St. Mary, 3:30 AM).

Angelus: 8 AM, noon, sunset: 9 or 12 strokes (doesn't matter) on Kbira, the large bell on the Stage-right tower (except noon which is always 12 strokes).

Tal-Orazzijoni: they call it Sieghax Leji (hour of night). The guide recognized the bell between sunset and Tal Imwiet 9 PM.

Tal Imwiet: slow, 9-12 strokes, Kbira

Mota Tal Hamis: 7:45 for 10 minutes. Gdida, Tas Salib, Fostanna, Kbira. Feast of St. Mary, Tal Angeli added as first bell.

Either I did not ask about the Friday mota or the guide couldn't get across to the sacristan, more likely the former. Both the guide and the sacristan were showing some signs of impatience with each other. The guide said he should know the names of the bells, and he borrowed a scrap of paper from the sacristan and wrote out the names. I thanked both of them, and gave the guide 50¢, which is too much, but he had tried very hard.

Later I spotted the fact that Dominicana was not used or mentioned in any of the ringings, like Stella Maris at Marsaxlokk.

I went back to my car and decided I would drive back through Mdina and Hamrun, because I wanted to try to get a case of drinks at the Farson's plant. It was very crowded at the junction of the Mosta-Mdina road, with many parked cars, walking people and karrozzin. I think there was a race going on. I drove into the Farson's plant but the man at the gate said it was too late to buy drinks there. I should go by the police station in Hamrun and ask for the Farson agent there. Naturally, I didn't see a police station in Hamrun.

At home again, I fell out for a nap, and took the rest of the evening off, which is why I am typing these notes on Wednesday night.

Critique: I am not getting full information, either because

1. I forget to ask
2. I ask but forget it later (not so likely- my memory is pretty good)
3. I am not asking the right person
4. The person I am asking is impatient and I chicken out.
5. The person who is translating can't get what I want.

Comment: If you want anything like a detailed survey out of this you are going to have to make a list and back track.

Backup to Sunday, July 16th: (The wedding and reception at Zejtun):

Johnny brought Norma back from the sea about 5:30. Norma came in with Mother Scicluna. Present was Carmen, the unmarried younger brother, his chubby girlfriend, Johnny, Paula. We talked for a while, stuffing drinks into them. I noticed Carmen's girl- really must be his fiancé- was quite free about touching his legs. Norma brought Mrs. Scicluna a bunch of flowers from the garden. They left about 6:20. The wedding of Johnny Maniscalco's bother began at 6. We decided to skip the mass and left Hal Tmiem at 6:45. At Zejtun, we parked behind the church and were directed to the reception hall is called the "Alexandria Hall." It was located on the second floor, a long narrow room with red folding chairs and red drapes. A row of columns separated part of the left side of the room. Plastic flowers decorated the walls.

Plan: (ex. 22)

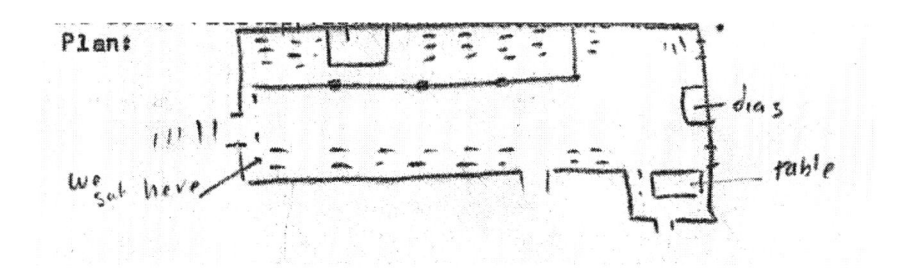

[Diagram showing floor plan with labels: "Plan:", "we sat here", "dias", "table"]

We were quite early; there were only a few people there. The band was lounging over by the bandstand, three young men playing an electric organ, an electric guitar (sharp) and a trap set. A fourth person played an electric bass. After a while they began to noodle and tune. The electric guitar remained sharp all the time we were there.

People continued to dribble in. A set of young boys were cutting up over to the right of the band. Thy made much ado about smoking cigarettes and parading in and out. Finally, the bride and groom arrived, followed by the Inglesi ladies, Joan Grundy, Moria and several more. Everyone applauded. It was the Maniscalco brother with the side burns and mustache, the one who smoked the pipe and who had done most of the directing on the occasion of taking the boat out of the boat house the Tuesday before. The bride was a slender girl of about 18, pretty in her gown, but with some pimples down the right side of her chin. We went up to shake hands soon, because none of us had eaten and the dish of ice cream and the cookie were going to get would be welcome. Johnny's sister was one of the bridesmaids. The positioning was: Johnny's sister, the bride's father and mother, the bride and groom, the groom's father and mother, and another bridesmaid.

The ceremonies, as far as I observed them, followed the same order as the wedding of Johnny Scicluna's brother in Zabbar. The photographer pushed everybody around. The food order was: Ice cream and an oblong cookie, almond cookies, scotch or vermouth (dance photo here), candy (cut the cake) champagne, sandwiches, then raisin cake.

Norma wanted to move around to the corner, as the band was quite loud. Standing over by the table, I was accosted by a neatly dressed young man who said he was Johnny's cousin (1st) and who said he was interested to know why I had been at the church with a camera and tape recorder. He said he was doing work at the university under Aquillina in linguistics and launched into a lengthy discussion of his paper, which was a study of color perception. He was quite excited about the fact that for the Maltese, sea blue and "sky" blue are entirely different colors. He made me very uncomfortable because he insisted on standing very close and spitting at me. I backed away several times but he followed. Finally I crossed my arms on my chest to keep him a little further away. It was true that it was hard to understand because of the band and the conversation, but my territorial proxemics had been invaded and I was most annoyed. Then, after he drove his magnificent paper into the ground, he asked what my study was. I launched into a purposefully technical description I'm sure, went right over his head.

About that time, Marcia rescued me and I excused myself. Marcia, Norma and I then left for home.

Earlier, Mary and Lena Grech came in accompanied by a Twiggy type girl whom Lena introduced. The three girls sat across the room from us. The male- female division was complete. No one got up to dance at all. As we were leaving, the girls were beginning to twist by themselves in front of the bandstand. The guitar was still out of tune. I learned later that they had made the band turn its volume down.

Back to:

Tuesday, July 18

My appointment with Blind Boy in Ghaxaq was at 10:30. Marcia and Norma's dresses were ready to be fitted, and they wanted to go for a fitting this morning, but Norma didn't get up and Marcia drove me to Ghaxaq alone, promising to pick me up at 11:45. She was a little pissed and drove like a fiend.

We were met at the steps of the church by Blind Boy, and a friend, who were already waiting for me (of course). I had taken the tape recorder and unloaded it now from the back. I had to explain that Marcia couldn't stay and I would not have the car. Blind Boy said it was a shame, because he wanted to show me the small church he had mentioned last Sunday. He said my wife would enjoy it also, and I explained she was my sister. Marcia and I had agreed upon this bit of fiction beforehand when we had moved with Norma to Hal-Tmiem.

I learned later that Blind Boy's name was Lawrence Dalli. Lawrence had already arranged everything. He had someone read him the inscription in the vestry of the church and had already typed it for me. We were to go to his house. The friend deposited Lawrence on my arm and we made our way down an alley to the right of the St. Joseph Band Club. All the shops and clubs were closed, by the way.

Lawrence kept up a stream of steady conversation about the alley, the age of the houses, etc. We arrived in front of a blue doorway and he led the way into a small courtyard. We were greeted by a large German Shepherd, and a smaller dog, both of which yapped. There were about 4 birdcages hung around the courtyard, the occupants of which also stared a commotion. Lawrence's sister and mother were there. The sister is also blind. The mother is a small woman in black with worried eyes. She spoke no English. The sister was quite fat and bobbed and nodded her head when she spoke and smiled all the time. It was pathetic to see Lawrence and his sister addressing one another, for they both fell into a kind of bobbing dance, like two birds. I did not hear the sister speak a word of Maltese while I was there. Lawrence's mother motioned us into a curtained room. Lawrence wanted to take me somewhere but I asked to see the typewritten page he had done. He produced a four- page translation of the bell ringing rules. I sat down and read it over, asking him questions about it. The mother produced some Kenny's (drinks) and biscuits.

Laurence had interpolated some explanations about the various feasts and occasions. It was a remarkable job for a blind person and I really appreciated what he had done, although I intended to check it as closely as I could. I asked if he would play his tape for me and let me record it, and he obliged. The taping took about 12 minutes. By that time it was getting close to 11:30. I tried to find out the names of the bells, suggesting that we go over to the church and find someone who knew. Laurence was most insistent that no one who knew was there. His mother understood the gist of the conversation and began naming bells, Carmena, Maria Ruzarja, Don Mercell, and I said "your mother knows," but he insisted that she didn't, so I dropped it.

Laurence insisted on accompanying me back to the street, because he wanted to show me a very interesting house. It turned out to be the house in back of the church, which was covered with lettering and dedicated to St. Mary. Laurence said the filigree decorations were done in snail and seashells by a former bus driver. The house was divided into three apartments. There were niches for statues and Latin inscriptions.

On our way up the street, I noticed a small boy making a trumpet like sound by blowing on a flat narrow stick on one end of which had been fixed a section of bicycle inner tube. The boy was holding the tube on the stick with his hand and blowing with the tube partially inserted in his mouth. Kind of what we used to call a Jew's Harp.

Laurence and I stood for a moment in front of the ally where his sister and mother had appeared. I think his mother was trying to get him to come back home. They left shortly and we went down the street to stand in front of a bar. All the bars had all opened by then. Marcia arrived in a minute and I thanked Laurence. Laurence still wanted to go to that church with my sister, but I explained we had some appointments and had to get back.

Laurence's address: 40 Don-Jusepp Naudi Alley, Ghaxaq, Malta.
Some observations:

The list in the church was in old Maltese, prepared by Joseph Naudi, after whom the alley was named. Laurence said his mother had worked as a maid for this man, the parish priest. The list was prepared in 1943.

As I checked the list, Laurence said many times that such and such was no longer done. He said the priest, will, many times, altar the bell systems to his own tastes. Many bell ringings were no longer necessary.

A mota (according to Laurence) can be rung on a single bell.

Laurence said the masses were held in Ghaxaq at 5, 6, and 8:30 AM- on Sundays at 5, 6, 7, 8, & 10. During bird hunting season, special masses are held at 3 AM for the hunters. The "passage" bird season is from the last week in April to the last week in May. The quail season is from the first week in September to the last week in October.

Formerly, during Lent, people used to fast on bread and water ("like Ramadan," Lawrence said). Now, fasting is done only on Ash Wednesday and Good Friday.

I spent the rest of the day (Tuesday) typing field notes. Marcia and Norma went out in the afternoon, complaining about the crowd of people out. About 5:30, I drove to Marsaxloxx to walk down the Quay and over to St. Lucian's tower. I had brought some letters to read and I wanted to be alone. The small pill-box on the cliff was occupied (I saw two pairs of feet), so I climbed over the hill to the road in back of the towers. Three cars were parked there. I climbed around the wall and out to the point where I read my letters and returned about 30 minutes later. One of the cars appeared to be empty. As I climbed up the hill on my way back, I saw some motion in the corner of my eye, and looked back to discover a couple having sex in the front seat. My reaction: not shock or envy, but that they really deserved a good cool bed and a bottle of wine. Poor people, hemmed in by culture, religion and rock walls.

Wednesday, July 19

I got up early, fixed some breakfast and left for Valletta. I had a time finding a parking place. I arrived there about 9:30. I had thought to check the morgue of the Malta Times to see if I could find anything about the prohibition of the Pater Noster bell. But I decided to check the Royal Library first.

When I arrived, I asked the attendants if they rememberd the Pater Noster incident. They did. One person said it was in 1968. Norma and Marcia said they thought it was around July of 1970, because it seemed to them that the bells in Marsaxloxx then had been rung far more often than at present. I checked all through July, 1970, but couldn't find anything.

A gentleman and a young girl stopped and asked if they could share the table. The man was about 45-50, and worked in the ministry of education. I think he was helping the young girl with some research. He asked my nationality, and I took the opportunity to solicit his aid. He remembered the incident, but the thought it was 5 or ten years ago. He suggested I go to the Archbishop and they would tell me. After pouring through 6 months of Malta Times, I was ready to agree.

I went back to the Archbishop's and spoke to Mons. Bonnici. He was most cooperative. He said there might have been a secular letter issued about the bells and that he would try to locate it for me. I was to return there Saturday about 12. He also said he had a document dated from the time of the French occupation prohibiting the bells. He said it was easier to find this, because it was historical. I said I would like to see this document as well.

Afterward I stopped in a small restaurant for an orange drink and a pastry. I had it in mind to buy some soap and typing paper but my gumption took over and I went for a look at St. John's Cathedral instead.

(ex. 23)

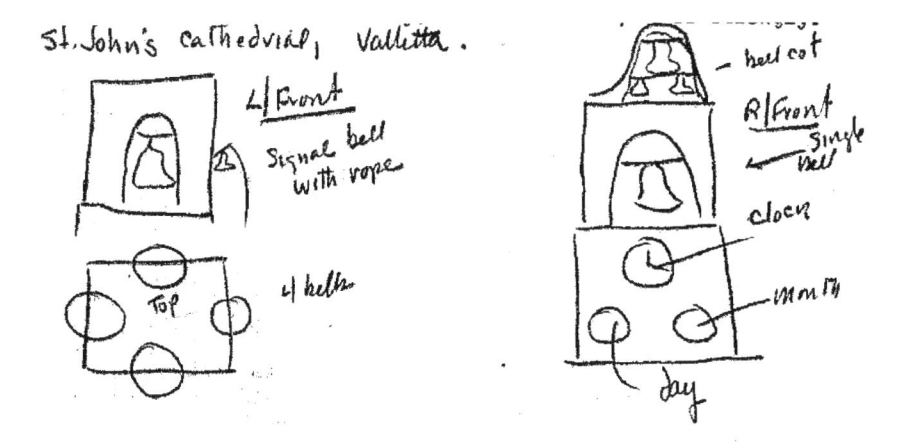

Foto 19, St. John's

    I walked up and down to make a sketch of the bells, but it was hard to see them because of the trees. I noticed there were repairs going on in the left/front tower. No one paid the slightest attention to me. I went inside and was directed to a priest upstairs in an office. The priest was busy writing in a small booklet and pasting some stamps therein.

    I had seen this taking place on the occasion of my first visit to Mons. Bonnici. When the stamping was finished- a small lady belonged to the book and she was very chatty- he turned to me and I asked him if there was someone to show me the bells. He gave me the usual spiel about going down stairs and finding the sacristan. He could not give me his name because there were several of them and he didn't know which one was on duty. I did manage to get the following out of him:

1. The bells of St. Dominic's and Lija are especially fine.
2. This man used to be the pastor at Floriana. He enjoyed the bells. Foriana was in a big square with no houses near, but he could see how they might be disturbing to someone living nearby.
3. During the day of the feast at Floriana, Motas were rung from 4 to 6 and from 8:30 to 10:30.
4. The tower at St. John's had been damaged and repaired during the war, but the recent earth tremor had made it loose again and they were repairing it.

I enjoyed talking to this man very much. He was kind of a middle aged DeGaul-like figure. He shook my hand and said "God Bless you."

At St. Dominic's, there were great movements of chairs and draperies inside and I judged everyone was too busy for me to bother. Besides, some chairs and crates had been stacked in the stairs to the front/right bell tower, and you couldn't get up. So I did my shopping, had a pizza, fought my way past a traffic jam in Floriana and went on back to Marsaxloxx, where I found both a Farsons truck and the milk man. As I was driving away (the milk truck was parked by the Grech apartment) Mary Grech came up. She said she had been swimming at Gozo yesterday and had some sunburn. She said after we left the wedding reception she danced with some boys. She only took some champagne, no scotch or vermouth.

Back home, I took a shower and a long nap. I began work on these notes again, but the Scicluna's came by and stayed until 10:30. These notes were finished at 2 AM.

Back up to Tuesday, July 18th: (yesterday)

Johnny Scicluna, Paula and little Paulo came by in the evening to see if anyone wanted to go to sea again Wednesday. Norma had a sun burn from Sunday and opted out. Johnny said "that's alright; if I catch anything I bring you some." I asked Johnny about the clock ringing system, and he knew it cold, and explained it thoroughly. He seems uninterested in my work on the church bells. Wednesday night, when he returned with some more sea eggs, he told many stories about the church and its preoccupation with power and money, of which he disapproves strongly.

Forward to:

Thursday, July 20^t

I got up late and fuzzy this morning. Norma and Marcia went off to Valletta. I drowsed around, took some sun and finally went back to bed. I got up about 4 PM. Marcia and Norma had returned and gone to bed. I loaded up my bag and split for Zabbar. I'm probably getting a little too collective about churches. Marcia made some inference to this in the morning. I feel I need churches in all quadrants. My intention was to cover Marsaskala, another fishing village (I thought) and then Zabbar.

Marsaskala was a bust. Evidently, it was once a small village, but the number of new buildings and apartments make it seem quite atypical, at least in comparison with Marsaxloxx. I finally located the church on the other side of a roundabout below what looked like a large school or institution. The church was new and unfinished and the bell towers had yet to be completed. I assumed they were going to build some towers because when I climbed up the stair there was a hole in the roof.

The church was in use already. A small old man came out of the church just as I as reading the bulletin board. I said "bon jeu" and he started talking to me in Maltese. First time I've ever been taken for a Maltese- no, the second time. Anyway, he switched to English when I did and said I could go in. I copied down the times of the Masses: Saturday: 7 PM, Sunday 5:30 AM, 6:30, 7:30, 10, 6 PM.

I followed a paraffin (gasoline) truck into Zabbar from Marsaskala. It is amazing how close everything is and yet how far away they seem. Sometimes the huge parish churches are only good city blocks away from each other, and yet so many dwellings, roads and alleys intervene that the distance or rather the sense of distance is fooled- i.e. one's sense of distance as "far" or "a good piece" or "near" is dilated.

The road took me directly to the church in Zabbar, which I remembered from the wedding of Johnny's brother. It is a very ornate church, decorated with more than the usual number of statues and curly-cues. I counted two large bells in the right-front tower and at least 7 in the left/front tower. The extreme left side of the left bell tower had four bells in it, and it looked like they were all supplied with external hammers of the type used with the clocks. Yet the clock (mounted on this tower) sounded only two notes a major third apart.

Plan of Zabbar Parish Church.

(ex. 24)

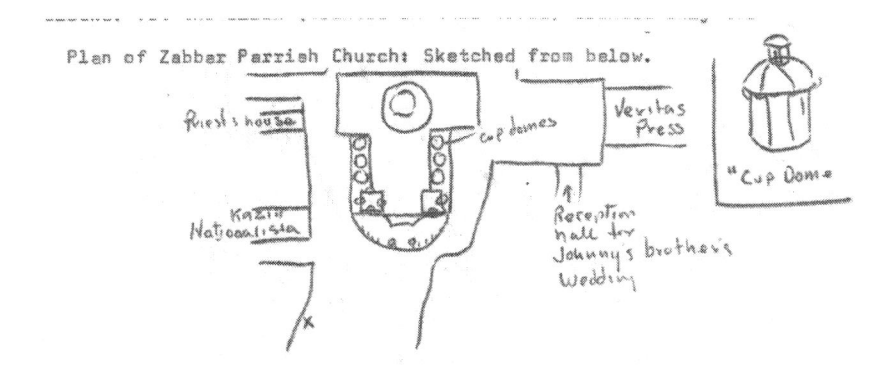

The bells in the left of the left/front tower:

I wandered about and took several pictures. No one paid the least attention to me, as usual. The bars were all closed and very few people were about. The church is situated at the SSW end of the town, which is laid out longitudinally along a main road. It is not at the center therefore, there were not so many people about.

It took me a good while to find the priest's house. I must have walked past it several times. The church itself was practically deserted. I rang the bell and a slender tired looking man of about 45 answered the door. He said to come in, that he was also waiting for the father. I went in, relieved to be out of the heat, and took a seat in the hall.

The parish priest's house was practically identical to the other houses I had been in, with a long narrow hallway and a curtained office. The only difference was that this house was a little larger and a little dingy. There was another woman waiting with the man. I took the opportunity to draw an elaborate sketch of the church in my notebook.

The parish priest appeared in about ten minutes. He was a squat chubby man with gray crew cut hair, rimmed glasses and a rather absent expression. The man and woman went into his office with him and emerged after a while. I presume they had gone in to get their God-stamp, or whatever. The priest said come in in Maltese (I assume), and I went in and introduced myself. I thought at first he didn't speak good English, so I slowed down my spiel and waved my fingers. It turned out he spoke and understood well enough, he was just a bit odd. His desk was piled with odds and ends and the front of his black gown was grey from cigarette ashes. He smoked incessantly while we talked. The cigarette waved up and won in his lips as he spoke and the right side of his front teeth were discolored from the nicotine. His name was Rev. Gius. Zarb (I found out later) and he turned out to be the local historian. Well, he had done a lot of research and published two pamphlets, one of which he gave to me. He was a pedant, very proud of having traced down the donors of various votive offerings in the Zabbar church. He said he had discovered an unknown tower concealed by the houses in a certain alley. The moats were used as wells. He had even found the holes where the hinges for the drawbridge had been. It was impossible to get him to stay on the subject of the bells. He had traced the ancestry of several of the bells. He said they had been melted down and recast several times, sometimes into fewer and sometimes into a larger number of bells. Two pages of one of his publications were devoted to the bells. It is in Maltese- must get someone to translate it for me.

Father Zarb repeated the story I had heard from Johnny Scicluna, about the "tongue" of a big bell falling off and not hurting anyone. The story is printed in the pamphlet he gave me, <u>20 Sena Ilu</u>, Veritas Press, Istitut Sagra Familja, Zabbar (1970). He also related how a painter had fallen from a scaffold and some men had come to get him, because they were sure he was killed. Father Zarb grabbed up his extreme unction kit and went over to the church, but the man was up and walking around, uninjured, and thankful his glasses hadn't been broken.

Another tale of Father Zarb's (which he related in his other publication) had to do with a small boy whose family was too poor to give the priest a chicken like the other families. Father Zarb said this little boy loved him so much that he saved a few pennies, bought a chick, raised him for a year and then presented to him. Father Zarb said he gave the boy a wristwatch for his valor.

While the good father was droning away on his researches on the knights of Malta in connection with Zabbar (and in truth he had done a detailed if pedantic job of sleuthing), I memorized a mota I heard ringing at 5:45, 15 minutes before mass. The two bells were tuned a fifth apart:

(ex. 25)

Father Zarb said I could go and find the sexton and get him to show me the bells, but perhaps it would be better after 6:30, because mass was about to start. I asked if I might return the next day instead, and he said fine. He did not know the date of the Archbishop's edict on the ringing of the bells before 6 AM. He did say that the Pater Noster used to be rung at Zabbar at 4:45, 15 minutes before the mass at 5.

Backup: The man from the education ministry and I believe also the priest I talked to in St. John's said the bells were prohibited except on feast days, which explains the 5 AM bell that woke everyone up in Marsaxloxx on June 18th.

I drove back home through Paola and Tarxian. When I arrived, I found Norma and Marcia seated at the dinner table with a heavyset young Maltese wearing a police uniform. It seems Marcia had to walk to Marsaxloxx to get some things for the dinner Norma had planned for Moria that evening. Marcia said she had told me on Tuesday, that Norma had invited this English woman to supper

Thursday, when she met her at the wedding of Johnny Maniscalco's brother last Sunday. The policeman had given Marcia a ride back to Hal-Tmiem. I had assumed all arrangements for the dinner were complete. Marcia and Norma were asleep in their room when I left and I hadn't wanted to wake them. I goofed, but it was a simple misunderstanding. Anyway, the young man (who seemed quite taken with Marcia) had proved a fount of information for Marcia who received a great deal of information on prostitution, which had been one of her projects this summer. The young man's name was Paul, and he said to come by the police station in Marsaxloxx if we ever needed any favors. About that time Moria arrived with Joan Grundy. I talked with the policeman for a while about driving and driving conditions. He said to be careful, because there were many bad drivers on the road who were not properly trained. In the days of the former government, people could bribe the police and get a driver's license without taking a test. Under the present government however, this had been stopped. A policeman he knew had been arrested and taken from the police force for this recently.

During the earlier conversation, he had repeated the sentiments we had heard from Johnny Scicluna, about how one respected and kept the faith of the religion, but how one was stick of poor men becoming rich priests with several cars and servants. After Joan and Moriah arrived, he said goodbye in the kitchen and Marcia showed him to the door. I rather had the impression he wanted to say goodbye to Marcia alone (!).

We went into the front room. Norma served drinks and we talked. Norma put away more than a few drinks, I thought. Supper was roast lamb. Norma carved, and chips of lamb flew onto the floor. It was very hot. After the meal I fixed some coffee for Joan and myself.

Norma had put on her Cockney accent as she does when talking to English people. I don't know what they think of it or why she does it. It embarrasses me. Norma spent three years in England, at the London School of Economics. I suppose an accent is catching. But In New Orleans I had meet a young man at supper, a native of New Orleans who had spent some time in London (in hot water) and who had the most affected British accent I think I have ever heard. However, he never turned it on and off.

After dinner I disappeared into my room. Norma got really soused and was getting on my nerves. I am a work addict and I wanted to get on with my notes. Joan and Moriah left about an hour later. I waked Joan- a little soused by this time and very cuddly; pity she isn't about 40 years younger- and Moriah, along with Marcia and Norma out to Moriah's car. After we had seen them off, I went back to my room. In a little while, Norma knocked on the door jam and said she had a bone to pick with me. She settled herself on the far twin bed in my room and lit into me for having gone off without asking if someone else wanted to use the car. She said I knew she was having guests at 6 o'clock and I had returned after 6, that I had insulted Marcia, and that I had been antisocial by retreating to my room after supper. She was laying down the law. She was putting her foot down; by God this was going to stop, etc., etc.

Frankly, I don't mind being reprimanded for a mistake. I had apologized when I came in However, I felt that I was perfectly capable of making an agreement, that Norma had no call to talk to me in that tone of voice, with that expression on her face and in those terms. I became very angry, but then I remembered how my father, a dedicated Mason, never lost his temper. I tried to explain that I had told them I was going out this afternoon, and they had said nothing to me about using the car. I said every time I sat down to try to plan the use of the car, she refused to cooperate. She never seemed to have any projected plans, and would often change her mind about any she had announced earlier. Everything I said fed her anger. She launched into another salvo and then asked if I understood her. I said I understood her that was the problem. She got up and stomped out of the room, her shoulders swaying from side to side. This is her "exit act" having made a final devastating remark. Effective, until you learn to expect it. Then she went into the living room, where I could hear Marcia trying to calm her down. They did one of their "Joseph" translation bits and I could hear Norma screaming and sobbing for hours.

I thought she was quite mad. You always had to tip-toe around Norma.

First Reaction: "I can be out of here in 20 minutes." Several people had laid bets to see if I could stick the summer out with her. She has alienated and driven away at least 4 of her Tulane students I know of. One of them committed suicide. But he was cracked to begin with. Norma has been leading up to the same scene with me for years, to get me to reject her. Then she can enjoy the fact that another trusted person has betrayed her. I watched her go through the same process with Tony B., the informant she and Marcia had employed two years ago in Malta.

My final conclusions: I don't mind being criticized when I have screwed up. But to go through that for a simple misunderstanding is not worth it.

I have put this scene in my field notes because it will color my relationships with Marcia and Norma and also my future work. I dislike trying to live with a person like Norma whom you never know when they are going to turn on you like that. Later I went up on the roof and thought for a long time, and then went to bed.

Friday, July 21

Friday, I got up late; fuzzy again. Norma came to the door and asked if I wanted to use the car, she and Marcia wanted to go off somewhere. The situation has continued in an uneasy truce. We are very polite.

That afternoon about 2:30 I borrowed Marcia's tape recorder and retuned to Zabbar. I wanted to record the Friday 3 PM bells for the Last Supper. No one was there; the doors of the church were closed and locked. At a few minutes to 3, two old men appeared and hastily unlocked the doors. It would have been better to go up on the roof for the purposes of recording, but there was no time. I recorded the bells from the churchyard traffic noise and all. The pattern was similar to the one I had heard and notated in Marsaxloxx, several rings on the highest bell, followed by bells in descending order.

After the ringing was over, I went inside the church and located the sexton, but alas he spoke no English. No one had "picked me up" in this deserted end of town, so I had no interpreter. I packed the tape recorder in the car and decided to look for the place where Guliano Cauci had had his shop: Ghayn Dwieli, which was between Paola and Vittoriosa.

I never located Ghayn Dwieli, because there were no signs and I must have passed right through it without noticing it. I decided to continue on to Vittorioso to see if I could rouse anyone at St. Laurence about the bell, which had supposedly been made from metal collected form the fields of the temple of Hercules at Marsaxloxx. I located the church without any trouble. Marcia and Norma and I had been there early one Sunday morning to look at a Palestrina book, at Father Gaberetti's invitation.

St. Laurence Church is located just above the wharves of the grand harbor. Directly in front of the church and slightly down hill is a small park. Below that, is a stretch of open wharf and then the harbor. To either side of the wharf are military dockyards, closed to the public. A large Australian Navy ship was tied up at the right wharf. I took a preliminary survey of the church and its bells and then snapped some pictures of the ship and the front of the church.

St. Laurence's had no clock, and I heard no clock bells, or any other bells ringing, except form a distance. There seem to be five bells concentrated in the front-left tower. The right tower was empty as far as I could tell. Inside, there were only a few people praying. Some men and boys were hustling about the altar with stepladders, adjusting or changing the tapestries. Not a priest in sight, even back in the vestry. There were plenty of clerical garments hanging around; a few black hats with broad brims and one room had empty glasses and some bottle caps on a table, but no one was around.

    I felt it was better to get to a priest before I bothered the sextons, who were obviously very busy. I went back outside. Over one of the doors, I noticed the date 1691. There was a square with some shops and bars uphill behind the church. I walked up and found an open bar, where I ordered a Coke. There were a few men already there, and they kept up a continuous argument all the time. The gesturing was interesting. When a point was to be made, one of the men would get up and go near the others and tap the table and wave a fist up and down with the thumb extended. Once I thought I caught the word "commando." I think they were referring to me. A bunch of British commandos had returned just last week and were observable everywhere. In Malta, they have not seen enough Americans to be able to distinguish between British and Americans.

    After about a half hour I finished my Coke and my pipe. I had gone to the square in hopes of getting picked up, but no one seemed curious or interested. I returned to the church, which was still empty of priests. I decided to wait in the park until 4:30 so I could go knock on the Parochial Office door next to the church. While sitting on the bench, I noticed two young girls sunning themselves quite lavishly on the wharf next to the gate where the ship was docked. One girl had her mini skirt up over her black panties. After a while, a young man drove out of the gate, and nearly lost control of his car ogling back over his shoulder. He pulled up and shouted something at the girls. They got up, arranged themselves, and went over. After a brief conversation, they both got in the car and drove off.

I waited until slightly after 4:30 and knocked on the office door, but there was no response. I finally gave up and drove home to a nap, supper of fish & chips (which Marcia and Norma had gotten in B'buga), and worked the rest of the night on my notes.

Saturday, July 22

I got up late- well, 9-ish (late for me). Marcia and Norma were off to do some shopping and they dropped me at Kingsgate about 10:30. This was the morning I was to return to the Archbishop's to look at the documents Mons. Bonnici was to have located for me. I had it in mind to shop for some gifts, but the city and stores were so crowded that I had little chance to look. Finally, I took a Coke at a bar on Zachery Street and then made my way to Archbishop Street and the office building there. Mons. Bonnici took me to the document he had located. It was in a folder in a room directly down the hall from his office. He was very cooperative. He said he had found an earlier document. The one he showed me was a large page printed in Maltese. It was so large it had to be folded over to fit into the file. It was about 10 x 14". The date was February 20, 1945. Mons. Bonnici said it was the only copy they had, and it was too large to microfilm. He read some of the text to me. The circular dealt with the daily cycle of bells and not just the Pater Nostar. I obtained permission to return on Monday about 9:30 and copy it. Mons. Bonnici introduced me to several priests here. They were all friendly and cooperative. Mons. Bonnici also gave me the name of a book to look up – Castagna: <u>Storja ta'Malta</u> – which I could find in the Royal Library. He said there was also another book that lists Maltese bells, but that he couldn't think of it right away.

People were rushing about, obviously in a hurry to close. I thanked everyone and said I would return on Monday. Mons. Bonnici said he was going on retreat the next week and would not be there.

I went to the Royal Library and asked one of the attendants to get the book for me. The attendant was a small, slender man of about 40, very dark. After a long while he returned from the stacks empty handed and went to look at the pile of returned books, where he finally located the volume I wanted. He said there were several editions, and he checked to see if this one was the latest. It was: 1890. In the back we found a list of foundries and a list of bells by Guliano Cauci. By that time it was almost 12:30. I had promised to meet Marcia and Norma at the "Bologna" Pizza Restaurant. I made plans to come back and copy the list and to look at anything else the attendant could think of.

The attendant was from Gozo, and he supplied the following information about bells in Malta and Gozo.

1. There is a Major Koli Abab of Central Hospital, Victoria, Gozo who is doing a study of Gozo church bells.
2. In St. George's at Victoria, there is a custom of ringing the smallest bell at 11 AM found nowhere else. It seems that the Knights had donated a cannon to the melted down for the bell. The only stipulation was that the bell be rung that the normal time that the guns fired (a salute?), 11 AM. The cannon was donated by the second Grand Master, Peter del Ponte (b. 1534, d. 1535).
3. Two Toxen bells, bells used to sound alarms on the walls of fortresses, are known to exist. One that hung on the bastions of Mdina is to be found in the small church of Taduna, which is located in Rabat, a little distant ("up the street") from the Roman Villa. The second Toxen bell is hung in St.

Julian's, located near the Sliema hotel. It used to be hung in the fortress of St. Angelo.

4. An Italian firm has supplied sets of fine bells, identical in tuning, to the following churches: Qala, in Gozo. St. George, Victoria, Gozo. Mellieha. At-Warel...(? Probaby Wardija), nr. St. Paul's bay.
5. At Wardija, the church called "Abandonata", was owned by a nobleman who loved bells very much. He used to go to certain feasts just to hear the bells rung. His inheritors, however, did not appreciate bells, and so he wrote into his will that the bells of his church were to be rung exactly as they were rung during his life. There is a young bell ringer there now whom I might be interested in consulting. This church is not to be confused with the church of St. George, which is nearby.
6. During a feast at St. George (Victoria), a young man whose father and grandfather had rung the bells took a whole day off from his factory job just to go and ring the bells as his ancestors did. He received no pay.
7. The great bell at Birkirkara was not made by Guliano Cauci, although he once supplied such a bell to the church there.

The pizza lunch at the Bologna Hotel was terrible. The service was off and the pizza dry and skimpy. It has been good before. The place was full of Inglesi.

At home, I continued to work on my notes. Marcia called about 5 or 6 to remind me about the wedding of Salvu Ragel's daughter. I had thought it was Sunday. I dressed quickly and we drove to Johnny Scicluna's in Zabbar. Johnny and little Paulo were waiting in front of the alley (Johnny Scicluna, 7 South Alley, Prince of Wales Square). We want inside for a drink. Mary and Paula were there. Johnny brought out a letter he wanted Norma to type, a recommendation for his brother, Gilly – the one I call "Smiley"- who was considering taking a job in Libya. When we left, Johnny and Paulo rode on the scooter, Mary and Paula with us. Mary seemed a little less boisterous than usual, probably because of the death vigil now in its second week for their mother in Qrendi.

The reception was held in De La Salle College, outdoors on a large veranda. When we arrived, the bride and groom were already there and the food was savory, not sweets. This was a high or upper middle class wedding with many finely dressed couples and several priests and brothers. Several singers were there besides Johnny- Ta Vestru- the smiley man who had sung with Ragel and Johnny on June 3rd at the Rediffusion, and two others. After congratulating the bride and groom we found some seats on one corner of the veranda and settled down. Ragel and his wife were not present. Norma said it might be because the mother was going through a "my poor baby" fit. They did appear later on. Ragel came over and spoke with us. Johnny said he has both money and "fame," because he is known everywhere as a contractor and singer.

The band was set up on the stair landing. It was a smooth, professional group and played mostly rinky-dink music until the sun went down. When the band began to play some folk-like dances, several round dances developed and a conga line formed. As usual, the children were given full freedom of the place and ran up and down and back and forth. The single exception being Paulo, who was not allowed his freedom by either Mary, Paula or Johnny. Why? Does he get into trouble?

Later we tried to get out, but the bride caught us and asked us to wait, she was going to change her clothes and return in a minute. Ragel and his wife had left earlier. We went back to our chairs for a while, but finally got up and left anyway.

Earlier, the bride had come around to where we sat with pieces of the wedding cake- it was white frosted raisin cake. She apologized to Norma because she said she was only supposed to serve the men.

Later when Ragel was talking with us, he called over to the groom to come over and serve the women.

Johnny called my attention to some lyrics the female vocalist was singing during one number… "hobla de hobla do"(!)

I saw Father Zarb descend the staircase late in the evening. Johnny said his nickname was "Artiste."

When we finally extracted ourselves and the car, and got Paula and Mary in the back seat – they had wandered off on the trek out. I think one of them ran into the bride. We went to the open-air bar at Marsaskala. Johnny led the way with his Lambereta. At the bar we had not been seated for more than 5 minutes when Johnny's younger brother drove up in his white Anglica and joined us. He sat next to me and called my attention to some "ladies" at the next table. I could see only long hair and slacks. I wondered what he was referring to. After a while, I noticed the arms and the hips and the hands as well were not characteristic. They were young men, homosexuals, enjoying a drink with an older, balding man with a mustache who was very loud and boisterous. Johnny evidently knew him, for they exchanged some jokes.

After a half hour or so Norma invited everyone to Hal-Tmiem for some whisky and we made our way there. I was very tired and sleepy by then, and so was Paula. Mary and Paulo had been dropped off at Zabbar. Finally, after about a half hour or so, everyone decided to leave.

Some observations: Marcia said this wedding blew Boissevian's theory of a classless society to hell. It seemed also that the order of food had been changed. I believe Johnny said that ice cream had been served first, (then the meats and sweets and cake) and then ice cream at the last again. Maltese ice cream is coarse and not too good.

I should have spent more time in the libraries and offices before doing so much field hopping. There was much more information there than I supposed at first. Also, the Rediffusion should have been consulted, once the project took shape.

Sunday, July 23

I slept late and had a late lunch also. Mostly, I worked on these notes and wrote some letters. The weather had become very hot and the wind has stopped blowing. Marcia and Norma went out and reported the traffic was very heavy in the late afternoon. Johnny and Paulo came on Johnny's scooter. We all got in the car and took a long drive around B'buga to the festal in Zurriaq. Johnny guided us to a field above the town and we parked the car and got out to watch the first kaxxa infernale (fireworks). Johnny said there was some kind of weed that was good for driving mosquitos away, and found some in a field. Norma took copious notes. Soon the petards started (the mortars that lunched the explosives into the air) and then the 21 petard salute, the "kaxxa". Only the last petard was a dud. After the kaxxa (which was spectacular enough in the broad daylight), we made our way downhill to the church. On the way I asked Johnny about the final "bloom" which always accompanied the patterns of two and three "flares" of petards- the "pow- schloom, schloom", ….. "bang" type- and he said it was to end, to say it was over: punctuation. I thought this tied in with the final emphatic stroke in the mota Sammuit at St. Paul's in Rabat had been mentioned, and also with the formal announcement that one is leaving- "immoru."

The pijja at the church was very crowded. The statues and banners again reminded me of some pagan movie set. I took some pictures. Johnny led us into the band club for some drinks I tried to pay, but failed. Outside again, we strolled away from the church and went downhill through some narrow streets to the street in front of the church, and then walked back. I took many pictures. About half way up we met Johnny Maniscalco. Back at the square, Johnny took us into another bar- the other band club, I think. The two clubs were St. Catherine's and Queen Victoria's. It was the titular festal of St. Catherine. In the club, Johnny met a friend and they argued about who was to buy whom a beer. Johnny won as always.

Afterwards, we left and made our way out of the square back the way we had come. The bells had been tolling all this time, in a steady mota pattern that had commenced while we were back near the field. I could distinguish three bells, a high bell, one a 4th lower, and one a 5th lower than the first. Amidst all this, a band started playing. When we left the bar, a small chorus of girls had gathered to sing with the band. Two microphones on either side of the band led to outdoor speakers on either side. We picked our way across the street just as the Saint's statue was almost at the church. In fact, we had to step into the confraternity's marching lines to get across. They didn't seem annoyed.

Back at the field, we waited for the firework colors and the final kaxxa. Johnny had bought a large square of candy he cut apart with my new Maltese knife and passed around, it was so sweet that it hurt my teeth. About 5 or six boys were hanging around, cutting up. They set fire to some boxes in a field and started throwing them around until Johnny stopped them. They behaved in the most obnoxious manner, shouting, picking gourds from a field and throwing them, and arguing with some little girls. No one paid much attention to the boys; they were allowed to behave as they would, with the exception of the burning boxes. They sure made a mess.

The kaxxa, the fireworks grand finale, was spectacular as usual. When it was over, we got in the car and drove over to have chicken and chips at B'buga, in the bar next to "Charlie's." Returning home, Paula and Johnny left on the scooter and we went to bed.

While we were waiting for the first kaxxa early in the evening, groups of people passed us, going down the road to see the festal. A young couple (Maltese) pulled up in a car and talked with Johnny and Paula for a while- did we meet them in Qrendi on Paula's roof?

Once, a strange girl with a loose red cotton dress and a carrying basket, shuffled past us. Her black hair was disarranged and hung over her face. Her feet and ankles were wet. She swayed from side to side as she waked and seemed to look at the pavement. Several times she stopped- and then continued. I don't know if she was blind or mad- perhaps both.

Monday, July 24

Marcia and Norma dropped me off at Kingsgate, Valletta about 9:20. I had been told to go back to the Archbishop's around 9:30. I made arrangements with the girls to meet at the fountain about 2 PM. On my way I had to stop at the public lavatory on Strait Street, just a block up from Archbishop Street. I had gone there once before. The attendant was different this time. He guided me to a booth, handed me three lengths of toilet paper and asked for some money, a shilling. The washbowls at the other end of the room had no towels, nor was I offered one.

At the Archbishop's I found that Mons. Bonnici in the Secterjiat office was away on retreat. Instead, I walked into the archives and found that one of the priests there had already taken the folder out for me. I settled down on a table with a florescent lamp and began to copy the Maltese. From time to time, other priests came in and talked to me briefly. I met the priest I had seen in St. John's, who seemed so friendly. He shook my hand again and wished me luck. Once, a priest working in the archives who sat at a phone and a typewriter to my left said, "everyone is admiring you because you are taking the Maltese." This man seemed to be in charge of a little worn stamp, because several women creeped in with pieces of paper for him to stamp.

It became obvious that the document was not the one that prohibited the Pater Noster bell. After I had finished copying it, I took some photos and then asked the priest if there was not a circular that contained the information I desired. He took out another large folder and poured through it for quite a while, and then as more priests came in he asked their advice. One of them went for the Vicar General, the wizened little man I had seen before who wore a red skullcap. At one time, there were 6 people sifting through the documents. Finally, one of them asked me to come back on Friday. As I left, they were still hunting.

One of the priests had given me another book to look at in the Royal Library: Giovanni Faure: Storia ta'malta u ghaudex, Vol. 4. Emilio Lombardi, Sliema, Malta 1916. At the library, I obtained this volume and the P.P. Castagna, Lis storia Ta'malta bil Gzejer Tahha Vol. 3. Both contained lists of bells made in Malta. The small man from Gozo- I think his name is John Bezzina, (from a name plate on the desk)- was very busy and had little time to help me. I asked if I could get a photostat of the pages I wanted, since the list were extensive and the library would only be open for another 45 minutes. I was taken to see the assistant librarian- Father Gabrietta once more. Father Gabrietta greeted me, but said the man who did the photos was not there. I asked if I could take some photos with my camera and he said why don't you? So I did. I hope they come out.

I asked Father Gabrietta about the bell in St. Laurence church which was said to be made from metal from the Hercules temple. He said it was true, from the door handles. He mentioned the name "Cassawa" – "Cas-say- wax" in some context. I think it is the source of documentation. I told him I had been to St. Laurence the other afternoon, but found no one. Father Gabrietta said he wished he had been there. I should come about 9 AM some morning and speak to the sacristan.

A note on the books- I photographed pages 249 and 250 from the Castagna, and pages 1201-1203 from the Faure. The dates for Guliano Cauci (Giuseppi u Giacchino- sic) are 1835-1896 (Bormliue). His father was also a bell maker. His name was Salvadore Cauci.

I had a leisurely lunch at the British Hotel, over near the harbor and then arrived back at the fountain at Kingsgate, about 1:45, where Marcia and Norma were already waiting for me.

That afternoon, I had intended to go back to Ghaxaq, but it was just too hot, so I skipped it. That evening about 9:30, I took the car and drove to Marsaxloxx. I was quite uncomfortable and seemed like I couldn't breathe or wake up. I parked the car on the Quay near Tony's Bar and walked down towards the sports club, which was all lit up. Almost to the club, I met Mary, Lena and their skinny (Twiggy) friend. Lena and Twiggy were walking arm and arm. We stopped to talk for a while. I accompanied them back to a place on the quay in front of "Casa Grech", where we sat down to talk. Mary, Lena and their friend had walked from B'buga. They do a lot of walking, evidently. The Sunday before, they had been at the feasts at Zurriaq, but hadn't seen us. Mary had been practicing her harmonica. She still could not play "Oh, Susanna." Lena said she was mad at me for giving her the tiny harmonica, because she was driving her crazy. After a while Johnny Maniscalco wandered up. From time to time people came up listened for a while, said something, then left. I think Johnny's younger sister also joined us, together with a skinny young boy in shorts and undershirt and a mop of curly yellow hair, whose name was "Fenka"- he turned out to be the son of a singer who lived in Marsaxloxx.

Johnny, Lena and Mary talked about Finn W. a lot, the Norwegian who had accompanied Marcia and Norma to Malta on their first trip. They liked Finn because, they said, he made them laugh, made them happy. They said he was a very kind man, always ready to help people. They thought his walk was very curious. He was a tall fellow and walked with very large steps. Lena said that was why she had asked me if I were drunk that night on the quay (July 1st?), because I was walking funny. I was relieved to hear it- don't know what I was doing, perhaps ambling from side to side in my loose sandals. I had thought I was perspiring and it smelled like whiskey.

On the walk down to the quay, Lena and Mary kidded me about those words I had mistaken. I said I thought Mary knew all the dirty words and was twisting my mistakes. I told them about the song I heard at the wedding of Salvu R's daughter last Saturday- the one with the hoblado- habladee refrain. Mary and Lena laughed. Twiggy didn't understand until Mary explained briefly in Maltese. Then Twiggy went "arrrrrrgh" and bent over, laughing. It must be very bad indeed.

Back on the quay the conversation turned to ghost stories. They said the cemetery at San Gregor was haunted. Mary said that when there is a death and she is called to go to the house to baby sit she doesn't do it because, she said, she still sees the dead person in her mind. I think this ties in with the proverb that to think about someone, is to call them. Lena was very unconformable and asked that we changed the subject. We talked about fishing, and I said the only ocean fishing I had ever done was in Panama, where I caught a small shark once.

Lena told about a joke she had played on Mary one rainy Sunday. Mary was working for some Inglesi and Lena told her that they told her to tell Mary to go and babysit. Mary was quite unhappy about it and she was expected to sleep in. So Mary got her pajamas and grouched up to the flat. She was let in and she went into the front room and began to read a book. In a while the lady came in to ask why she had come, and Mary said to babysit. The lady said she had not called her. By that time it was raining quite hard and the husband took the car out of the garage and drove her home. Lena said she laughed so hard her stomach ached. Mary was mad, but she got over it.

Lena explained they had so little to do out of the ordinary that they liked to joke and laugh. She related a story about a Lampuka she had given to an Ingelsi lady she had worked for, and who kept it for a long while and then gave it to another lady, whom Mary worked for. Mary told Lena, and Lena kidded the first lady, who wanted to know if the other lady had told her. In fact she went to the other lady but the other lady said she hadn't told Lena. Finally, it was revealed that Mary had seen it and told Lena.

About that time a young man walked up and began amusing everyone (but me!) with his comments and jokes. His name was Fenka. Fenka really had them in stitches, - he didn't know very much English, only a few words. He stayed there with his arms folded making wisecrack after wisecrack, some of them directed at me. He had a dog that was fat and when he fed it, it became thin. If I was a doctor, how could this be? Etc. Mary explained that he made them laugh a lot, and he didn't mean any harm. From the above, it is apparent that the Maltese like to wisecrack a lot. This is confirmed by many other experiences. The wit sometimes revolves around making plays on words, like Shakespeare, or upon practical jokes or humorous incidents. A study of Maltese humor should be done: it is integral and it keeps the tempest going in the teapot.

Lena also said she didn't like to use the work "Makkok"- which means monkey- i.e. sneaky clever- because it was a word used by country people. If she used this word in Valletta, people would know she was from the country. I had been showing off my Maltese, and the word had come up. They were very amused and went to some trouble to try to help me. Kbira, for example, had a hard "G" sound I have never gotten, except by accident. "dqiq"- flour- is a word the Inglesi cannot say. But I can say it OK – it has a "t-ii-uh" sound.

Shortly before I left Lena and Mary, their mother came out and seemed to say it was time for them to come in. It was about 11:30 by then. Lena didn't pay much attention and the mother went back inside. I stayed for a while longer, and then left. I shook everyone's hand in mock courtesy, and returned to my car.

Tuesday, July 25

Monday night before I went to bed, I managed to dislodge a gob of wax in my right ear and shove it back against my eardrum where it stuck. I slept badly and got up late. Marcia and Norma had arranged to rent another car for themselves, and I took some milk and cookies and was ready to depart, when Johnny M. showed up with an acquaintance, Mickey, a guitarist singer who was, according to Norma, a failure at both. He was a short squat man with enormous gestures and a very loud voice. He liked Noma very much and invited her and us to a party he was giving Saturday. Another man and his son accompanied Johnny and Mickey. We sat at the breakfast table and Norma served them tea. I took the opportunity to make myself some coffee. My right ear was stopped up and I was very uncomfortable.

When they left we got in the car and dropped by Joan Grundy's in Marsaxloxx, who knew of a doctor who had taken a pea out of a little girl's ear without hurting her. Joan's car was not there, so Norma drove up to the Wiggeries where the American family from Carbondale was staying. I ran in and asked about a doctor from the Mrs. She and the maid gave me the name of Dr. Portelli, who made calls in Marsaxloxx from Paola, and of Dr. Borg in Zejtun, who had done the pea removal. We drove to Mr. Fenech's garage in Floriana where Marcia and Norma's dark grey Triumph was ready. They had decided to rent their own car since I had become so busy with my work on the bells.

I drove back to Zejtun and parked in the square to the right of the church. I went into a chemist's shop. They directed me to Dr. Borg, around the corner at the blue door just before you get over into Kamikaze alley. He also mentioned another doctor who lived in back of the church, because he said Dr. Borg was very busy and there were probably a lot of people waiting. There were three people in the small hallway outside the office. I decided to wait. There was no receptionist or sign or anything official. A staircase probably led to his living quarters upstairs.

In a few minutes, the doctor came out the door with a black bag in his hand and left in a hurry. I assume it was an emergency call, because I waited a half-hour and he never returned. Finally I went to find the other doctor (Dr. Zammit) who lived several doors down from the parish priest in back of the church. He was not there. I was informed by a young lady at the door to come back at one o' clock. I returned to Hal-Tmiem, fit to be tied. I forced myself to calm down, and fixed myself a late breakfast. I arrived back at Zejtun a little after one. A man in a business suit and a woman had just pulled out of the stony parking lot behind the church. As I pulled in they waved and drove back to the lot. I parked and got out. The couple came back to the door. The doctor had just stared to leave- he had waited a few minutes for me. He was on his way somewhere, was there anything he could do quickly? I explained about my ear and he took me into his office and looked at both ears, checking to see that it was only wax. He gave me a prescription for eardrops and told me to use them and return at 5 PM on Friday and he would wash my ear then. Or, he said, he would be glad to call where I lived. He said he made a call in the area of Hal-Tmiem and had seen me sunning out on the roof. He recognized me. Well, after all I don't think there are any other beards in Zejtun at all.

Dr. Zammit left in a hurry. I walked for a while, trying to find a chemist's shop that was open, but I knew it wasn't likely, and it wasn't. I drove back home in low spirits, very angry with myself for having poked my ear again. Inside, I was so fed up with not hearing anything, I decided to try an experiment with the hose on the bath tub nozzle, a short rubber affair for washing the hair, I suppose. I removed the nozzle and adjusted the water temperature and then proceeded to wash my own ear out. On the second try the gob of wax washed right out, much to my relief. It worked so well I did my other ear, also successfully. Now I think won't have to go to the damn clinic every time the wax builds up in my ears and wait for half a day. Eureka!

That afternoon, since my humor had returned, I drove to Gudja church. The church itself was a little smaller than Ghaxaq. The bells were contained in a tower to the front/right of the church, in an extension of the transept. The front towers contained no bells at all. This is rather unusual in my experience, especially for an older church. B'buga and Santa Lucia, for example, are new limestone block churches on the same plan with a single belfry on the front/left. Gudja church was quite old, about 300 years. The bells may have been in the front towers and then removed to the extra tower when it was constructed c. 1840-60. The architect was an Englishman, William Baker. The street to the front/right of the church is named after him.

I took some photos and did a reconnaissance of the circle of the houses in the immediate vicinity of the church, but did not find a priest's house. As the parish priests are not always from the town in which they priest, and since they are allowed to live with their families, some of them live a distance away. There were several bars open, but I decided to let the easy ones go and try the Band Bar. The Band clubs always seem as though they should be restricted to members only, and yet they are open to the public just like every other bar. The La Stella Band Club was just to the left of the church. I walked up a short flight of steps and went in. A group of younger boys were lounging in the hall. I asked if I could get something cold to drink and a lad of about 20 with dark hair, sideburns and shorts got up and served me a Coke in the bar in the next room. I remained in the bar for a while, looking at the pictures, then worked my way back into the hall were the boys were sitting. The rediffusion (radio) was playing "Knock 3 times…etc." and I took the occasion to explain what apartment houses were like in the US, and why the pipes could be hit. We talked about the band for a while. Several of the boys played instruments. I told them I played a French horn. They youngest boy also played this instrument. They said there were two bands in Gugja. One of the boys said this was the best. Another boy explained that the boy who had spoken was a supporter of the club. I told them about my work on the bells, and asked if I could find anyone who could take me to see the bells. The dark haired lad and the young boy jumped up immediately and said, sure, come one.

Over at the church, I waited with the young boy outside. There was no sacristan there. The boys talked back and forth for a minute through the door, and then I was taken inside, where to my surprise I found that the older boy had gotten up on the cornice, some fifty feet in the air and was climbing over to the choir loft! He clambered into he loft, disappeared down the stairs up there and then unlocked a door at the bottom from the inside so we could climb up.

(ex. 26); Gudja

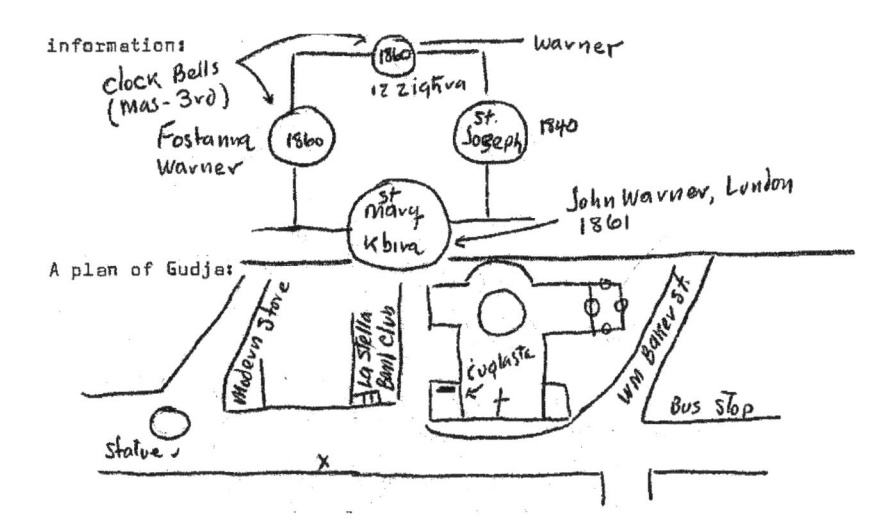

information:
clock Bells
(mas-3rd)
Fostanya
Warner

1860
12 zighva
St. Joseph 1840
Warner
John Warner, London
1861
St Mary Kbira

A plan of Gudja:
Modern Store
La Stella Band Club
cuglasta †
Wm Bakev St
Bus stop
statue
x

I took several pictures. We went to the front/ left tower where I could see the cuqlajta fixed to the back of the railing. We then went back down the stairs and I began to ask about the mota patterns and the Friday 3 PM ringing. The younger boy said his Sacristan had made him a practice board, and he cast about in the rubble of chairs and poles at the bottom of the stairs, but could not locate it. They said there was an old man in the village who rung the bells for the festal- he was a "professional" and had received medals for his work. He also rang the bells for other feasts.

Back in the church we paused in the choir loft in the rear. There was a cabinet for organ pipes, but no organ there. The boys explained that an organ had been planned at one time but had never been installed. Both the boys showed considerable knowledge about the church. The older one said he used to be a choirboy and knew every nook and cranny in the church. I learned that an orchestra sometimes plays in the choir loft, but never the bands. We went back downstairs and the boys took me in back of the altar. Up on another loft were the remains of an old upright organ like the one I saw in the cathedral museum in Mdina. The younger boy scrambled up some back stairs and opened the painted front of the case (peeled red and gold). The pipes within were fallen about inside. The boy took one of the smaller pipes out and blew upon it and asked me if I wanted it. I said no thanks.

I learned that Gudja was the "mother" church of several other villages which eventually became parishes in their own right: Tarxien, Kirkop and Luqa. The original parish church was very small and still to be seen over to the right of William Baker Street.

Evidently, a church is never torn down. The single exception might be at Mosta. The huge dome of Mosta church was said to have been built around the original church, which was then dismantled and the rubble carried out through the door. All in ten days.

The older boy said the prime minister had once prohibited the ringing of the Pater Noster bell. After examining the old organ and the new electric one just in back of the altar, we went back outside. I thanked the boys and left them at the band club. I told them I might send them a picture, but they didn't seem terribly interested.

Some other things in passing: the conversation in the band club got around to fireworks as it always does sooner or later in Malta. Once of the boys said that at Lija, which produced the best fireworks in Malta and which also sold to other villages, the fireworks plant there was "like a palace," it was so clean and orderly. He also mentioned that fireworks makers have to buy an expensive license, because there were so many accidents handling the raw black powder of the petards (the mortars).

I checked on the Friday 3 PM ringing – it seems to be similar to Zabbar and Marsaxlokk: an additive pattern from highest to lowest.

Leaving Gudja, I passed back through Ghaxaq and decided to try to photograph the list of bell ringings that Laurence had translated for me. I let myself into the vestry. There, I found a group of 10 or 15 small boys, and an older man. I asked about the framed list of bell ringings attached to a post there. The man kindly took it off the post and out into some sunlight for me to photograph. The boys swarmed about. One of them was wearing a scout uniform and I asked if they were scouts. The man laughed and said they were the choir and he was the director. I thanked them and as I left I said "sing sweetly," and the boys giggled and shouted things to me and to each other.

Back at the house later on that evening, we were invited over to Joan's for a drink and to meet Moria. As we were leaving Hal-Tmiem, Marcia squashed her thumb trying to lift the heavy garage door. I had offered to do it, as always, but she acted like she didn't want to let me do it, she had to prove something. We went back in the house and got her hand wrapped up in ice cubes and towels. At Joan's, other remedies were applied. When Moria arrived we talked for a while, then drove out past B'buga to our favorite restaurant: it was closed. Then we made our way to a place in Marsaskala called Arthur's, where we consumed swordfish steaks and two bottles of wine. Afterwards, Moria was dropped at her house. Joan insisted on being dropped in front of Tony's bar in Marsaxloxx, so we left her there and returned home. Except for Marcia's thumb, which was still painful, It was a delightful evening.

Wednesday, July 26

Another three-church day: Mellieha, Lija and Berkakara.

I managed to get up reasonable early, breakfast and get out of the house. My plan was to visit the Wardija church near St. Paul's bay, the church John Bezzina had mentioned when I was in the library. I then planned to do Melliha and then either Lija or Birkakara on the way back.

A bazzar was on in Zejtun. I drove past and parked on the road and then walked back to inspect. The main things sold were cloth, vegetables, cooking utensils, and clothing. I bought a pair of green shorts from a man who said to try them at home and bring them back Friday if they didn't fit. They don't.

I made my way through Hamrun, took the turn off to Birkakara and passed through Mosta, where I stopped for a Coke and some picture film. I took the turn off for Wardija. It was one of those narrow roads between two stone fences with a water pipe down one side that you see everywhere. The only exception was that this road went up the side of a hill. I am not sure that I ever found the church I was looking for. I found an old chapel connected to a larger building on top of one hill. It had only a single bell. Bezzina had said it was called "Abadnonada" and this one sure was. There was a lovely set of trees and the wind made rushing noises through them. Some locust-like insects made sawing noises. I took some pictures and decided to retrace my steps back to a crossroads. I took another road and finally came upon a sumptuous mansion with a chapel and bell tower. The tower was surrounded by a wall, and the gate was locked. The inscription on the gate said "La Sultana" – it did have a rather Moorish cast.

I gave up and made my way back to the main road and drove around St. Paul's bay to Mellieha, up through another set of trees and into a maze of narrow streets. I had a hard time finding the church, which ought to have been sticking out above the rest of the buildings and wasn't because the town was built on a hill. I finally caught sight of the church on a street down below me and drove back down some very steep hills until I came out just below the church. I couldn't find a street in that maze to get me back up to it. I always found myself heading out of town. So, I turned around and parked in a shady park below the church and wound my way on foot up several flights of stairs until I came out upon a broad street with the imposing church at the end. It was here all the time, but darned if I could find it in the car. Takes luck.

By that time it was almost 12 and I was quite thirsty. I took the last picture off the roll of black and white film I had in my camera and went into a bar and bought a Schwepps from a young man. As I reloaded my camera, we talked about America and my impressions of Malta.

Just as I was finishing my drink, a darkly tanned boy of about 12 came in the bar. I got up and asked how I might get into the church to see the bells, and the boy volunteered immediately. He said we must hurry before they closed the doors. The 12-noon Angelus had just gone off- I was counting the very slow strokes.

Inside the church, the boy led me up the usual 999 steps to the tower. I was glad to see he was more out of breath than I was at the top. Some men were working on the roof and some steel cables were strung across the bell tower entrance.

There were 4 large bells in the right/front tower, plus two smaller inverted metal bowls that were used by the clock. They were tuned a major third apart. The boy pointed out that the "tongues" were bound to the inside of the bells by greased leather thongs, because once several men were ringing one of the bells the tongue fell out and made a large dent in the floor of the tower which they had to cement over. The boy said the men had fallen to the floor when the tongue came out and hit the deck.

The left/front tower contained a single huge bell that was rung from downstairs by a complicated cable and pulley system. There was an unusual cuqlajta standing in the tower. It was large wooden box, about 5 x 3, painted gray and standing on wooden legs. There was a hole in the top. This particular instrument worked on a barrel and pin device. A handle turned a cylinder inside that had metal pins or projections around it. The projections lifted up blocks of wood and released the one at a time making a noise.

Returning downstairs, the boy took me into the vestry to show me a glass case with tubular chimes pitched to the tones of the bells. Each chime was tagged with the name and weight of the bell it represented. The bells had been made in Milan, Italy and installed in 1914:

1. San Francisco: Do. 2 x 46 ratlos.
2. San Guiseppe: La b, 5 qantar, 65 ratlos.
3. San Anthony: Mi b, 12 qantar, 94 ratlos.
4. San Paolo: Do, 2i qantar, 57 ratlos.
5. Maria Victoria: 1a b, 42 qantar, 61 ratlos.

(ex.27) Foto 20. Meillieħa cuqlajta

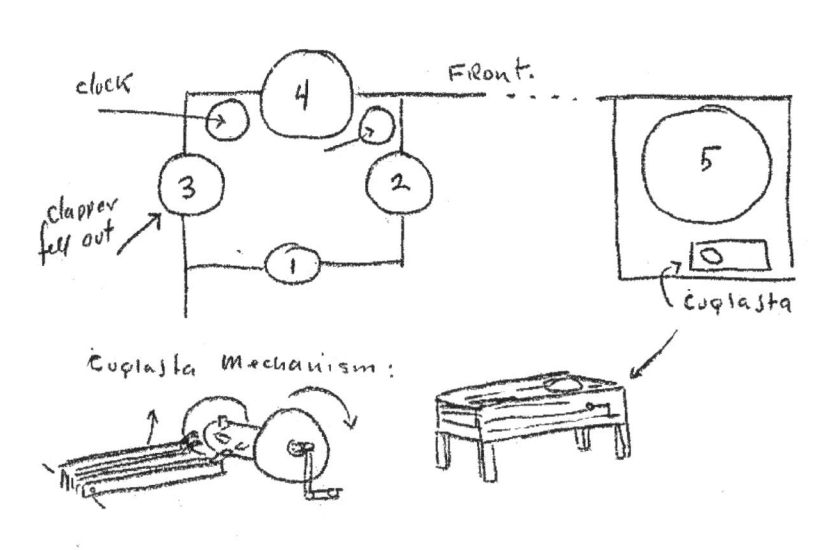

115

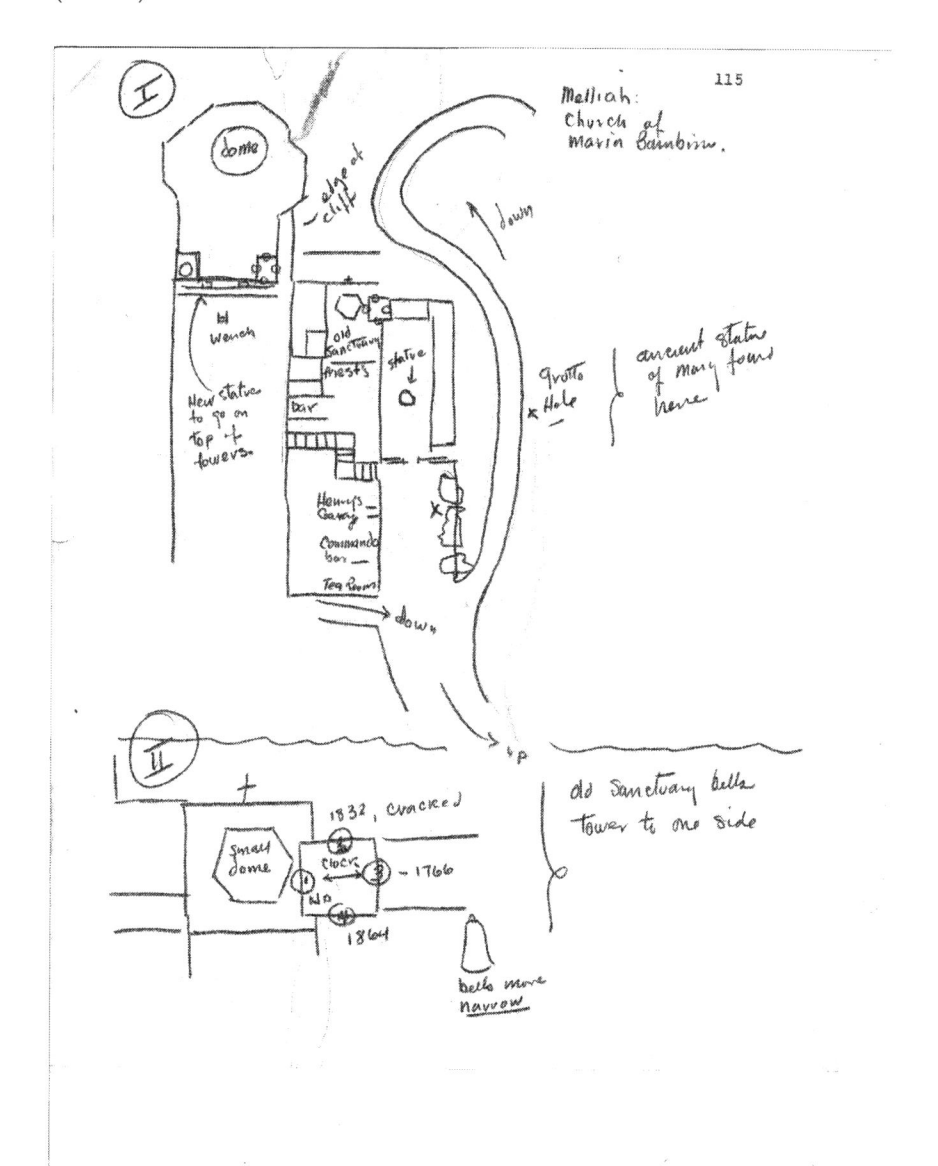

Melliah:
Church at
Mavin Bambien.

I

dome

edge of cliff

wench

New statue to go on top of towers.

Old Sanctuary Priests

bar

statue

Grotto × Hole

ancient statue of Mary found here

Henry's Gang
Commando bar
Tea Room

down

↑ down

II

1832, cracked

small dome

clock — 1766

No

1864

old Sanctuary bells tower to one side

bells more narrow

Foto 21 Meillieha Bell & boy

I had noticed a smaller church off the side of the larger church that had a small bell tower. The young boy had promised to show it to me on the way back. He had checked inside a house next to the bar before we had left, I presume with the priest or one of the priest relatives. After we saw the tuned chimes in the vestry (he had actually opened a small clock on the wall to extract the key for the case so he could open it to strike the chimes softly for me) we went back outside and down the steps. The boy told me the Archbishop had said that Mellieha had the most beautiful front of all the churches in Malta. In the street in front of the church was a large capstan or wench. Two white stone statues were waiting to be hoisted up and placed on the very top of the tower we had been in. The men working on the roof were taking down some stone caps and making some room on the top of the front/right tower, which had some scaffolding around it. In the front of the church we had stopped to examine the huge spool of steel cable they were going to use.

Foto 22. Meillieha: older church on hill below modern church

Foto23. Meillieha main church

The boy popped back into the priest's house momentarily and then led me through a garden and across the roof of the smaller church whose entrance was down on the level below. He said it was called the "sanctuary" and it was perhaps a thousand years old. The details of this bell tower are shown in ex.29. The front bell was chipped on the inside edge. The boy said it had been turned around. He said some men had been ringing the bell and some other men had been passing below; for a joke, one man grabbed the other man's hat and threw it at the bell, where upon a large piece flew out of the rim. The boy said it was because the rims were under so much stress when they were rung that it was possible to damage them in this manner.

The boy then took me out on the roof that extended over to the side of the tower and bent back to form a long rectangular courtyard with a small statue in the center. He seemed concerned that I couldn't clamber over the railings, but I had less trouble than he, because my legs are longer.

The boy explained that many years ago a boy lost one of his sheep. When they went to look for it, they found it had fallen in a deep hole. Down in the hole they found an ancient grotto with a small statue of Maria in it. They took the statue out three times, and three times some agency removed it back to the grotto, even though they placed guards around it. They decided to leave it in the grotto, after that.

After we had clambered back across the roofs and made our way back to the bar, I gave the boy some money and told him to buy some drinks for a friend. I think that is acceptable with boys. He didn't seem offended. I walked back to the square where I had parked my car – it was just outside the courtyard. I went into the "Commando" bar and got a ham sandwich and a Coke from the woman who ran the bar and sat down to write some notes. I noticed the woman and her daughter were pretty busy almost all the time I was there, restocking the candy displays and picking up the straws and bottles off the tables. Maltese bars are so small that if you didn't pick them up ever so often it would make a mess.

When I finished lunch (we had been invited to Johnny S's house for supper and I was warned not to eat so much), I went out and sat on a shady bench for a while, and then got in the car and drove back through St. Paul's bay and took the road to Lija.

Foto 24. Lija "Folly"

At Lija, I went through the usual maze and wound myself eventually into the square in front of the Lija church. I parked the car near some houses and got out to take some pictures and do my thing. Down the street in front of the church was a fancy "Tower of Piza" in miniature. I walked down to examine it and then returned to the square to sit down on a bench in the shade. I hardly the chance to write the word "Lija" at the top of my notebook page, when I was joined by an elderly Englishman and his friendly black dog. His name was Mr. Lang, and he had been a minister of education in Northern Nigeria. He had retired and lived here in his "Tudor House" behind us.

Foto 25 Lija Church

I believe I mentioned before that many colonial government people retired to Malta rather than endure the weather in England. He had lived there now for 6 years, in his "Tudor House" in Lija. He told me the following:

1. The square in front of the church had been occupied by a private palace that had been removed to make the square.

The tower down the street ("folly," he called it) was left over from the estate.
2. I noticed the Lija busses always had "C Lija" over top of the windshield. Mr. Lang said he thought or had been told it remained from some word like "casa" that denoted a town. It was pronounced like an aspirated "h."
3. I noticed one of the two clocks on the church was not telling the correct time. Mr. Lang laughed and said the one on the front/left was painted on, because the church was Baroque and they insisted on symmetry, but didn't see the necessity of having two clocks. I looked closer and sure enough the hands were painted on, at about a quarter to twelve. Mr. Lang said they usually had this time on the fake clocks, because it was the Angelus time, when the farmers were to come in for lunch.

Decorations were already going up for the festal in 10 days. Some poles and green posts were up and the electric lights had been strung over the front and the dome. Some dark red murals had been painted on the flat surfaces on either side of the door. Altogether, the Lija church was clean, well kept up and quite attractive. I ask if there was someone in the church to show me the bells at this hour. It was about 2 PM and only some men and boys were about, painting the front left door of the transept. Mr. Lane said these people were only workmen, and that Father Alfred Xuereb, the parish priest (who was born in Lija- it being highly unusual for a priest to be assigned to a church in the same town in which he was born) was not about at this time. Father F. was at Marsaxlokk a number of years ago and had risen rapidly in the ranks.

We walked over to the church and made inquiries. The sacristan was there, but evidently he didn't have the keys, or would not show people around without permission. I drew a sketch of the bells and got their names and dates. Mr. Lang suggested I come back later or even better, late the following day when they would begin the novena for the festal, the "nine days" before the feast.

I thanked them all and went back to my car accompanied by Mr. Lang. We exchanged some pleasantries. He was very friendly, and I said I might return the next day (I didn't- am sitting here typing these notes instead).

ex.29

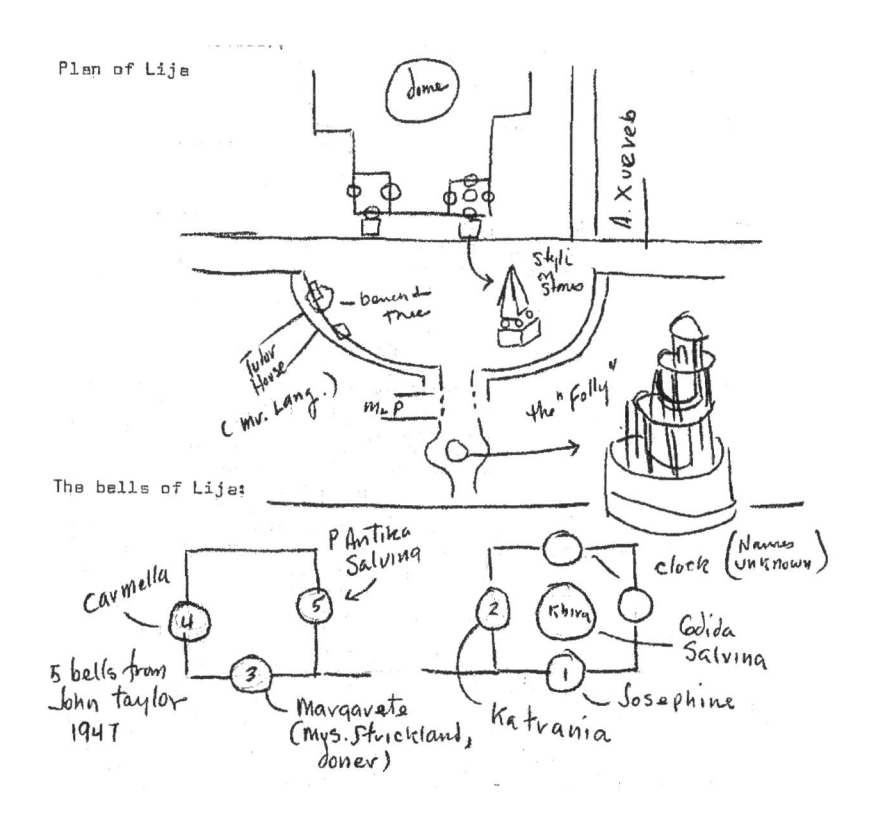

```
Plan of Lija
```

[Hand-drawn map showing: dome, A. Xueveb, Skyli m Stows, bench & tree, Tudor House, (Mr. Lang.), Mr. P, the "Folly"]

```
The bells of Lija:
```

[Hand-drawn diagram of bells labeled: Carmella (4), P Antika Salvina (5), (3), (2) Kbira, (1), clock (Names unknown), Godida Salvina, Josephine, Margarete (Mrs. Strickland, donor), Katrania; 5 bells from John Taylor 1947]

After leaving Lija, I went to Birkakara. Don't ask me how. I saw on the map that the church was located off to the left (north) of the main road, and so I did several passes through the incredible maze, always coming out in the fields on the other side of the town, until I found the church in the center of a large square. That much space was like an oasis in a desert, after creeping through the rabbit warrens of the Maltese maze. Actually, I parked the car as close to the church as I could manage and then walked the rest of the way. It is always a pleasant and inspiring sight to suddenly turn a corner and be confronted by the magnificence of the Baroque architecture of these buildings. The B'kara church was quite large, and I spotted the monster bell in the right/front tower right away. I took some pictures (under the direction of a passerby who showed me a good position) and then strolled back to the "Charlie Chaplin" bar on the corner. I picked this bar because it was crowded and had a lot of older men sitting in front. Inside I got a coke and later took and Ice cream. Some men were playing cards over to the side and got very loud about it. I took out my notebook and drew some sketches and noted down what Mr. Lang had told me. Once some girls in mini-skirts came in to buy something and departed. I was surprised that girls would go in a bar, but I purpose it is not too unusual.

Here a theory about the pretty girls of Malta. School is over at the age of 14 unless some examinations have been taken to go on to a higher form. After school is over, the girls blossom out and begin to look for boys and husbands. Every visual aid is employed – miniskirts to makeup. The Maltese are already very handsome people (although a little narrow in the hips), so that the girls from say 14 to 23 or so are very attractive. After the girl had caught her husband and is married, the goody rags are stowed away and the girl becomes a modest housewife, stays at home and bears children. Therefore it is quite rare it seems to me that you see an attractive girl over 23-25, because they are all married and living at home, or else they have married Jesus and are living with the Sisters. Besides, the Maltese grow old very quickly and the waistline bulges from the bread and noodles, the skin wrinkles and the shoulders sag from housework duties.

I was not picked up at the bar, so I wandered into the church. Back in the vestry there was absolutely no one around. I heard some keys clinking out in the church and I hurried out until I located them hanging from the waist of a slender little man whom I took to be the caretaker. I questioned him and waved my hands, pronouncing the words "campienella" and "qniepen." With a little English on his part, I got across to him that I wanted to look at the bells. He said "All right" and led me to the left/front tower and unlocked the door there and also one more on the second landing. I was allowed to continue by myself, my first solo on the roof of a church.

(ex.30)

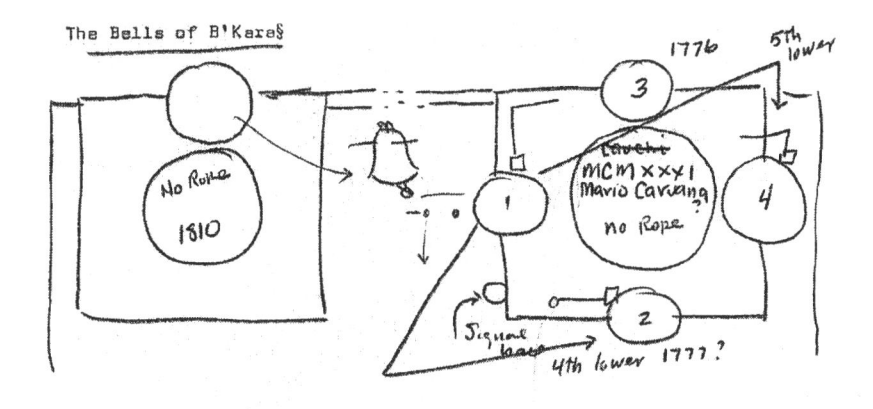

The Bells of B'Kara§

[hand-drawn diagram of bell tower layout showing: large bell labeled "No Rope 1810" on left; bell #3 labeled "1776"; bell #1 with notation "MCM XXXI Mario Cariana, no Rope"; bell #4 at "5th tower"; bell #2 labeled "Signum bass, 4th tower 1777?"]

The markers and dates were difficult to read on the bells, as usual. The big bell in the front/left tower is a monster indeed, it must be 8' across at the bottom and the clapper is about as tall as I am. Neither this bell nor the large bell in the front/right tower had a rope that lead downstairs, but only a short length for ringing in the tower. The other bells had greased leather thongs binding in the clappers, but not the two largest bells. I snooped around the roof for a while and took some pictures. I left, fearing that the sexton would think I had departed and lock me in. I looked for him downstairs but did not find him – hence the sketchy quality of my information here.

By now it was 4:30 and I was beat. I went back to my car and drove home in exactly half an hour.

At seven, we drove over to Johnny's. Marcia had gone to the hospital (St. Lukes) and had her hand x-rayed and bandaged. It appeared to be a hairline fracture of the thumb. She was really grouchy all evening, but I couldn't blame her. She told me once while she was studying in Germany, she stepped off a street car and fell down and twisted her ankle. People started to come to her aid, until she started swearing in German, whereupon everyone turned away, disgusted with her foul humor.

At Johnny's we had huge plates of Timpana. Timpana is kind of like lasagna, only with vegetables and without the tomato sauce. Johnny's brother, Nanu (Smiley) dropped by to return an octopus hook he had borrowed from Johnny. He was tired and disappointed at not having snared an enormous beast he had been diving for. Later, Mary Abbar (Paula's sister) and a male friend (don't know who he was- young man about 23 or so- a relative?) dropped in. They had just come from the mother's house in Qrendi. Johnny told some of his stories while stuffing us with sea eggs, cantaloupe and wine. He doesn't believe in ghosts – says someone has some business; whiskey; contraband and he wants you to stay away. Norma said later that the farmer's pragmatism wouldn't allow superstition in this particular form. Johnny said he had a dog once and they went hunting and the dog disappeared and wouldn't come when he called. He finally found him eating his way up inside a dead pig and he shot him and left him in there. Johnny was quite disgusted and showed it by scowling, pulling down on the corners of his mouth and waving his right arm in a wide gesture.

We toyed with the idea of going to Marsaskala for a drink, but it was late and Marcia pleaded that she wasn't feeling good, so we said good night. I kissed Paula's hand and she seemed very pleased.

Johnny walked us out to the car where we thanked him again. He said "I do anything for my friends" and nodded.

I took another wrong turn on the way home. We had a pleasant ride back towards Zejtun through the mazes. We met no cars, fortunately.

Some backups: Mr. Lang in Lija told me that he once had a naval captain for a guest during a festal. After the fireworks were over the old seadog took his pipe out of his mouth and said no wonder the Maltese were able to endure the siege in World War 2. I thought it looked like they were ready for the next one. Wonder how long the fireworks have been going on- any connection- influence from WWII?

Thursday, July 27

Got up at 7:30 this morning and drove early to see Mons. Prof. Colliero at the University. He wasn't in- his secretary (who was) said he was out of the country but would return tomorrow. I ought to call 36451 ext. 260 for an appointment. I decided to drive back over to Victorioso, and had a time of it. Funny, I made exactly the right turns the first time I went, but this time, I got turned around twice on the way out and once on the way back.

Inside the church, they were lowering the canopy over the altar and dragging out some new drapes and decorations to fit on it. Some women were polishing brass in the back. I went up to the older man there – the rest were teenagers and young boys- and mentioned Father G.'s name and asked if I could be shown the bell tower. The sacristan said sure, and delegated one of the boys (who seemed a little stupid- probably the only one he could spare), to take me up stairs. At St. Laurence, all the bells are in the front/left tower. There are six bells. I could get no information from the boy so I went back to the sacristan and got the names.

(ex. 31)

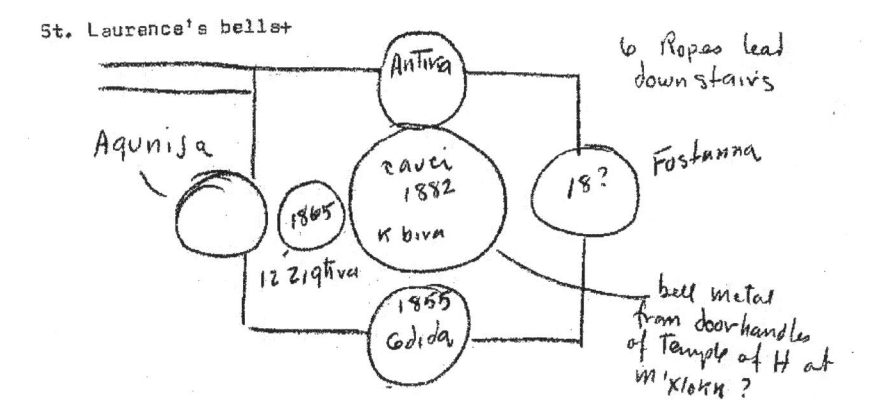

[Diagram: St. Laurence's bells+ — circles labeled "AnTiva", "Aqunija", "ravei 1882 / K biva", "1865", "12 zightva", "1855 Godida", "18?", "Fostanna"; annotations: "6 Ropes lead downstairs", "bell metal from door-handles of Temple of H at m'xlokn?"]

By then it was only 10 AM. I was tired from the day before, and so I drove back to Hal-Tmiem for a nap and a snack. Marcia and Norma were gone, over to the hospital and then to the post office.

I have spent most of the time since then typing these notes. It is now 7:20 PM.

Thursday night we went out to supper at Max and Tony's MacDonald (Casa Malinda, Delimara Road, Marsaxloxx). Moria ("Tara") was already there with her dog. Max and Tony are a delightful English couple. Norma became infatuated with them when we met them on the 18th of June at Joan Grundy's house, before proceeding to the dinner party at the "Americans" from Carbondale. I was particularly taken with Tony, (yes, the wife); her fine beauty and exuberant charm has increased with her years. Max and Tony met during WWII and were married in Egypt. Max had a large farm in Kenya that he was forced to sell by the government. He then bought and ran a hotel in Scotland for six or more years before retiring to Malta. They have two daughters and a son. After supper, we saw films of the African farm and of the game. When we left, Max cut flowers for the ladies. I got two carnations for my room from Marcia, when we got back.

Friday, July 28

Jackpot day at the Archbishop's Curia! When I arrived at the Chancellor's archives, I found he had pored over all his documents and had located four circulars that pertained to the ringing of the bells. The Chancellor said he thought there was an earlier circular dating from the outbreak of hostilities with Italy from around June 1940 that postponed the ringing of bells for the duration of the emergency, but he thought it might have come from the government requesting the cooperation of the church in wartime. He took my USA address and promised to mail the information to me (also the document from the time of the Napoleonic invasion) if he ran across it.

Roughly the documents are as follows:

- Cirkulari 460- 15 Sept. 1942: Pertains to the ringing of the bells as an experiment, in conjunction with the sirens.
- Cirkulari 474- 10 May 1943: Stern reprimands for the ringing of bells during processions. Parish priests and their superiors to be held responsible. Bell tower doors to be locked during processions. Evidently, the brunt of the war had shifted elsewhere and some semblance of peace was restored about this time.
- Cirkulari 476- 25 May 1943: Limited permission for the ringing of the Angelus- light strokes, and not more than 10.
- Cirkulari 481- 18 Aug. 1943: Full permission restored, but moderation recommended.

The document I had been looking for is Cirkulari 342- 17 Dec. 1968. It was contained in a longer document. The ringing of the Pater Noster was forbidden before 6 AM. I copied out all the documents in Maltese, thanked the chancellor, and then went to the Royal Library and check out Dec- Feb. of the Times of Malta. The earliest mention of the circular is dated Dec. 23, 1968. Subsequently, I found two complaints to the editors about bells still being rung before 6 AM. I copied all the references out and will append these and the Maltese documents to the field notes.

After lunch at the British Hotel, I made a trip to the MTV station in Gwadamana in case Joe Vella had my tapes ready. Joe was not there, but the attendant said he would be back about four PM. So, I went home for a shower and a nap. I returned to MTV about 4:15, but some technicians told me Joe would be back about 6. So I went back to Zejtun to see if I could tell Dr. Zammit my ear was OK- thought he might be waiting for me. I went into the waiting room of the office and found four other people there. I waited for a while, but gave it up when it appeared that business was going to be slow. I notice the people (two young boys and two young girls) waiting never looked at one another or spoke- they seemed embarrassed, or perhaps it was just my presence.

Friday evening we were to meet for supper at Johnny's, and so I drove again to Gwadamanga, planning to meet Marcia and Norma at Johnny's. I found Joe Vella in the control room, but he was all tied up and could not get the tapes for me. He said to return again in the morning and to see Vince Arrigo, who had the tapes in his office. Some days go like this. I got to Johnny's before Marcia and Norma. Mary cooked octopus for us- it was sort of good. The tentacles were firm but tasty. Afterward, Johnny said he wanted to make a contest with me. I had been attempting to open bottles with my knife and he set up two lemonade bottles. I was to open one, he the other. He used the lemonade to cut his wine. I opened mine on the first try (he said I could have three), much to everyone's surprise- (especially mine). Johnny opened his on the first time as usual. Everyone applauded when I succeeded in opening my bottle. Johnny said he thought his was "finer."

Later, we drove to the fine little openair bar at Marsaskala for drinks. Johnny started to drive his scooter, but left it behind when he saw we had two cars. I took Paul and Johnny in my car, while Mary and Paula went with Marcia and Norma. Johnny laughed and said "Men with the men and women with the women." He told me about the episode at the "Gozo Hilton" during Marcia and Norma's previous stay, when the landlady had insisted on separating the sexes.

At the bar I finally succeeded in buying a round of drinks!. Was it because I had mastered the bottle-opening trick?

Driving back to Zabbar, Johnny told me the roads thereabouts had been badly damaged during a rainstorm that had flooded the area. He laughed and said all the churches had rung their bells. This occurred about 20 years ago. After I left Johnny and his family at South Alley (Marcia and Norma had gone on by themselves), I took off down the road to Zejtun. A minute later I heard the put-put of a scooter, so I pulled over a bit to let it pass. It was Johnny, who waved me to a stop. He thought I had taken the wrong turn and was lost. I assured him I wasn't. He laughed and went back the other way. Actually, every time I had tried coming back from Johnny's to Zejtun this way I had gotten lost. It just so happened that I was drunk and low on gas, so that it is entirely logical that I did not get lost this time.

Back up: Johnny said earlier during supper that he would like to Indian- wrestle with me when we came to his mother's farm on Sunday.

Saturday, July 29

(scribbled:) "Left Malta"

POSTLUDE:

My field notes end abruptly on page 145, the last day I was in Malta. I had been typing them in London a day or so later. Somehow, I just never got around to finishing them, as I was feeling rather out of it since Norma's rebuke. Marcia was trying to be supportive, but was caught in the middle; there was little she could do to cheer me up. Anyway there was little time to do anything else than pack, try to restore the house, and trim the weight off our luggage. I had to fill up the gas tank on my rental car. Marcia, ever the pragmatic one, collected the beverage bottles (you couldn't drink the public water supply) and gathered the deposit. Together, we drove to an appliance store and bought a large revolving electric floor fan- a going- away gift for Johnny. Paula told us he had been having trouble sleeping in the still summer heat. My last duty was to drive my car to the airport for pick-up and drag the fan inside to present to Johnny as our going-away gift. He was delighted (and I was exhausted).

I don't remember much more about our departure, we were sad to be going, but we had planned to send some time in London before catching the plane back to the US, something I began to dread. I remember we sat a long time inside the plane waiting to take off. There was a brief layover in Naples. I remember the feeling of wonder at the sight of Vesuvius, the volcanic mountain covering a good $1/4^{th}$ of the landscape outside!

It was late in the evening when we got to Heathrow terminal in London. Norma had already made reservations. I was deposited at a quaint little hotel near Kensington Park. I don't remember where Marcia and Norma stayed. We were not talking very much. I didn't much care by then, I had resolved to make the most of the situation and enjoy myself. And I did. The Metro was around the corner and it was really easy to get around. During the next few days I traveled to just about all the interesting places, Westminster, Big Ben, Trafalgar, and Baker Street - Malta had toughened my walking skills. I took picture slides everywhere, even though it was cloudy.

Of course, the last day I was there, the sun came out!

Marcia did arrange for me to attend a play and a supper party with them. It was Norma's birthday and she had spent a lot of time there in school. There isn't much more to say. We flew to Amsterdam to catch our Tulane flight back to New Orleans, where I collected my car and belongings, spend a few days in a hotel in the French Quarter and then drove back to Greenville and my now-empty house.

So there it is; I was hoping at least I could publish an article or two on the clock and bell systems of Malta and the effect they had on the Maltese experience of time. Also, about the effect that cancelling the early bells had, because of complaints and the controversy it caused within the church. But I was asked not to publish anything of that nature by a high Church official, which took the wind out of my sails, so to speak. And the bitter argument and tongue lashing I received from the person I so admired and trusted, put me off my ambitions for further research in that area.

But all these things aside, my time in Malta broadened my understanding of human nature, and taught me how to cope with it in unfamiliar circumstances. It gave me the ability to train and prepare my students for coping with the great variety of human experience one encounters in unfamiliar places.

But also, and probably most of all, what a time I had!

I wish I could say Malta was the same as when I left it in 1972, but 45 years, almost half a century if you will, have passed. I never returned.

I can't say why, maybe it was the bad ending over being late for a dinner party (!), I don't know. Now I wish I had gone back, because things have changed so much.

I've been on the computer, on the satellite view. The churches are still there, but almost everything else has changed. In Marsaxloxx, a harbor once surrounded by barren hills, there are now houses and tall condominiums with large swimming pools and gardens. The roads are wider, better paved. The harbor still has a few painted boats, but now is crowed with small pleasure boats and yachts. The quay where once the fishermen gathered in front of their dwellings and mended their nets is now crowed with double rows of open-air stalls full of straw hats, scarves and tourist souvenirs. Tony's Aviator Bar at the corner seems to have been replaced with a classy restaurant, and the street is now paved with glossy stones. A large metal statue of a boy carrying some fish stands before the old common pool where you could skin your fish for supper, very artistic. I can't find the street or the house where we stayed, called Tokai, on "New Street Off Pope Pius V Street". Nor was our second home, Hal Tmien, anywhere to be seen.

And I wonder about the singers, bravely challenging each other, with the guitars strumming away and the fans cheering them on and trying to record their favorite singer; is there still a Lucy's Bar somewhere for them to sing?

Maybe you ought to go over there and find out. Or me!

Ara wire!

"Happy he, who, like Ulysses, a glorious voyage made."
Joachim du Bellary
1512 - 1560

Otto W. Henry, Ph.d
Professor Emeritus
School of Music
East Carolina University
Greenville, NC 27858

Printed in Great Britain
by Amazon